LILLIAN E. TROLL is Professor and Chairperson of the Psychology Department at University College, Rutgers University. She is a Fellow of the Gerontological Society and the author of *Development in Early and Middle Adulthood* and "The Family of Later Life: A Decade Review," as well as numerous articles in professional journals.

JOAN ISRAEL, M.S.W., A.C.S.W., is a psychotherapist in private practice.

KENNETH ISRAEL, M.D., is a psychiatrist in private practice.

LOOKING AHEAD

A Woman's Guide to the Problems and Joys of Growing Older

Edited by

LILLIAN E. TROLL

JOAN ISRAEL

KENNETH ISRAEL

A SPECTRUM BOOK

PRENTICE-HALL, Inc., *Englewood Cliffs, New Jersey 07632*

Library of Congress Cataloging in Publication Data
Main entry under title:

Looking ahead: a woman's guide to the problems and joys
   of growing older.

   (A Spectrum Book)
   Includes bibliographies and index.
   1. Middle age women — Addresses, essays, lectures.
I. Troll, Lillian E.   II. Israel, Joan.   III. Israel,
Kenneth.
HQ1154.L65   362.6 '042   76-58475
ISBN 0-13-540310-3
ISBN 0-13-540302-2 pbk.

Special thanks are due to Lynne Lumsden, Mary Allen, and Jacqueline McGinnis
for their support and technical assistance in the preparation of this book.

To My Mother by Jeanne Muller is published here
by permission of the author.

© 1977 by PRENTICE-HALL, INC.
Englewood Cliffs, New Jersey 07632

A SPECTRUM BOOK

2   3   4   5   6   7   8   9   10

Printed in the United States of America

PRENTICE-HALL INTERNATIONAL, INC., *London*
PRENTICE-HALL OF AUSTRALIA PTY. LIMITED, *Sydney*
PRENTICE-HALL OF CANADA, LTD., *Toronto*
PRENTICE-HALL OF INDIA PRIVATE LIMITED, *New Delhi*
PRENTICE-HALL OF JAPAN, INC., *Tokyo*
PRENTICE-HALL OF SOUTHEAST ASIA PTE. LTD., *Singapore*
WHITEHALL BOOKS LIMITED, *Wellington, New Zealand*

Contents

We dedicate this book to our mothers —
Bertha Ellman, Lottie Lifschutz, and Mamie Freedman,
who helped us meet the challenges of life
with a sense of vitality, hope, and confidence.

LILLIAN E. TROLL / JOAN ISRAEL / KENNETH ISRAEL

To My Mother

Lady in white
she sat and ate an apple on the sofa bed
in her bare toes.
There were other times
sitting on a beach blanket
her children running noisily around
her skin bronzed, bringing out a healthy glow,
that she felt like a beautiful woman,
but one being eaten away
by something going on quietly inside.
Now the years have nibbled me too, she thought
like the grey worm fingering the fruit.
My children are parents
I can't call to them now
and have them run up to me
full of energy and runny noses
hoping they will blossom with all my dreams
as I sit in the lake wind
asking a question of the sunset.

JEANNE MULLER

PART I

Introduction

HOW WE STARTED

LILLIAN: *I want this book to take off both from gerontology as a science and the feminist movement as a hope for the future. I want to consider theoretical and professional issues and I want to stimulate some consciousness raising, not only for our readers but also because of my own hang-ups about being an older woman.*

JOAN: *You're saying, Lillian, that it's good to get involved in an area in which theoretical issues are personal.*

KEN: *I think we feel these issues in a very concrete way. As I get older, I am more interested in older patients. I think, "My God, that's really happening to me, too." I used to feel more helpless in dealing with older women than I do now. Part of this may represent some change in me, but part of it is that I believe there are different possibilities for older people now, for older women in particular— more than there used to be. I can think of them more as people, as individuals, not necessarily dependent on someone else—usually, of course, a man.*

LILLIAN: *Thinking of them as real people rather than as somebody's mother, or wife, or widow.*

KEN: *Well, I guess that's a way of saying it—being real people.*

They were always real people to me, but they were people with fixed and narrow limitations.

LILLIAN: *There was no clear path down which they could move nor any way you could help them.*

JOAN: *I guess in that sense I am involved in this from a very selfish point of view. I feel, as a feminist, that the work I have done in the woman's movement has opened more opportunities for women. Since I am 45 whatever I can do to open more paths for older women will benefit me in a personal sense. I suppose professionally I have always been interested in older people. I have been successful in my work with them and this has encouraged me to deepen my interest.*

LILLIAN: *I've been thinking about some of my feelings. When I came to Detroit I came as an older woman, about 50, and I wasn't used to it. There wasn't any transition. Nobody knew me as the Lillian I had been all along before. I was not used to being treated as a stereotyped older woman. It was three or four years later that I became aware of some of my anger about this.*

JOAN: *I wanted to write this book so that new information and changing viewpoints about older women could be gathered together in one place. This should be available not just to professionals in the fields; it should be written in such a way that all women who are growing older will be able to understand themselves better. Growing older has to do with the way we as women see ourselves. We feel we are treated as sex objects in both subtle and obvious ways. Much of our self-esteem is tied up with how we look, the way our body looks, and the whole youth bit. To feel we are not attractive anymore because we are getting older makes our self-esteem plummet.*

LILLIAN: *Well, that's always uppermost in my mind. Telling somebody my age is just—I find myself blocking it out.*

JOAN: *You know, I get a kick out of telling people I'm 45 because they say, "But you don't look 45." So, I say, "What's wrong with being 45?"*

LILLIAN: *Yes, but it may be hard when they don't say, "You don't look it!"*

JOAN: *Yes—that's right—I haven't reached that point yet.*

KEN: *I think the question involves how one grows aware of time, time passing. During some parts of your life you don't really think much about time. It always seems like there's a great deal of it and then very suddenly it seems like there's not going to be enough—and it's grappling with that apparent change that interests me.*

JOAN: *I think it is interesting that we've decided to dedicate this book to our mothers and I think maybe what has allowed us to do this is that all three of us have very active mothers. Lillian and Ken's mothers are both in their 80s and my mother is in her early 70s. But I think that they have used their older years. They are living a vital kind of life. They have struggled with the sadness of growing old in many ways. Loss of husband, loss of job, loss of health; but they have not felt overcome by it and I think perhaps this allows us to really get together and do this.*

LILLIAN: *If we had less effective mothers, we would be more crushed by our own aging and less able to think about other ways to grow old.*

JOAN: *Yes, they have provided us with models.*

Chapter 1

Poor, Dumb, and Ugly

Lillian E. Troll

The Western world is full of old women, many of whom are poor,
dumb, and ugly. They start getting old when they get married,
and many of them age very fast. By the time they are 30, and sometimes even younger, they start worrying about their fading beauty
and their poorer chances of catching or keeping a man. Youthfulness and attractiveness are mixed together in most people's
minds — you cannot be attractive if you are not young. And if you
can't be attractive, what else is there? Your children are gone from
the house while you are still under 40. Your husband is deeply involved with his career — if he is middle class — or maybe just hanging onto a job if he is not. You have been trained from birth to be a
housewife and mother, but most of that job is over while you still
feel young and strong. You can clean your carpets like a professional with the most advanced product of the chemist's art, or take
ten hours to prepare a gourmet dinner, but so what? You watch
your husband anxiously to make sure he doesn't propel you into
widowhood before your time, because with each decade over 40
your chances of finding another man get smaller and smaller. You
are cursed with health, vigor, and the prospect of a long life; and

Lillian Troll, Ph.D., is currently chairperson of the Department of Psychology at
University College, Rutgers, and involved in a study of changes in adult life. She has taught
Life Span Development at Merrill-Palmer Institute, Wayne State University and Rutgers, and
is the author of *Development in Early and Middle Adulthood*, as well as numerous professional papers.

you have no skills or savvy to help you deal with the management of economic affairs, such as getting a job or managing the lowered income you get after your breadwinner is gone. Because education was more important for the men in the family when you were young and because your life has been filled with repetitive trivia, you are apt to think on a simple-minded level. Even the pleasure of intelligent conversation or creative activity are likely to have been denied you.

This would not have been true at the turn of the century, when most of today's social security recipients were born. Then your chances of being outmoded or obsolete were minimal because you were more likely to die in what is now considered middle age, leaving children still at home, and never knowing what it is to be shelved. Since then, however, several powerful forces have combined to produce the old woman of today. Medical advances are perhaps most at fault. Instead of dying during one of her constant childbirths or at menopause, a woman can now live out a full life span, into the 70s, the 80s, even the 90s. Unfortunately, the men are likely to go before she does. The latest figures show a seven year differential in life expectancy between men and women. The life expectancy for men born in 1969 is 68 years; for women born that year it is 75 years. The life expectancy for men born in 1900, however, was 48 years and for women 51 years, only a three-year difference. This differential is increasing steadily, at least until now — everything we say about sex differences may be changing now, even life expectancy.

Other factors that have made today's older women obsolete are the trend to earlier marriage and earlier childbirth — a shift that occurred in the 1970s — and the decreasing number of children per family. If a woman gets married at 20 or 21 and has her first child within the first year of marriage, and if she only has two children, two years apart she will be out of a job by 40. This is particularly true if her husband meanwhile has become lost or has strayed and she does not even have a second honeymoon to turn to.

Because these changes are the result of historical forces such as population and health factors, they may also be temporary. Poorer health care, different attitudes toward education and jobs, or greater appreciation of the charms of older women on the part of old — or, for that matter, young — men, could all alter the circumstances of the older woman. Increased education and a more interesting lifestyle can make the older woman a more attractive person, at least to herself. The generation of younger women now stepping into jobs hitherto reserved for men may easily become a very different kind of old women—*not* poor, dumb, or ugly.

Until about two generations ago, few women had the good (or bad?) fortune to age. Too many of them died as they lived— "barefoot, pregnant, and behind the plow." They died in childbirth or from fevers, often compounded by exhaustion. They died with their aprons on. The health and lifestyle revolution of the past century, which has enabled so many women to live beyond their time of traditional usefulness, has led to the existence of redundant older women.

Like their mothers and grandmothers, most women alive today—most women over 35, anyway—have been trained from earliest infancy to be servants. Their status in society, their worth to themselves, their joys in life, were all intended to be derived from the value, status, and achievements of other people whom they serve: men. They have been taught that whatever abilities or accomplishments or charms they have are to be used for pleasing someone else—for obtaining a husband, for enhancing his successes (or at least survival), and for generating successful (or surviving) sons. Their role has been a universal and durable one. It is supposed to last till the end of life. Until recently, most women were socialized into believing that there would *always* be a man or men who would let women take care of them. Men needed them.

But unlike their mothers and grandmothers, most older Western women today are finding that this *isn't* a lifelong role after all. They have not borne children as long as their bodies were capable; their growing sons reject their services and their husbands want them more for recreational than for survival purposes. In short, they are in danger of becoming obsolete. They have lived beyond the point for which they have been prepared, beyond the point where they are necessary, beyond the point where they know what to do with themselves, beyond the point where anybody knows what to do with them.

Western, white, middle-class women today have had only a few children. They have had them when they were young, and close together, so that by the time they are 40 they have outlived their primary function of mothering. And marriages today have a high probability of ending in divorce. While younger divorced women find it easy to remarry, with each decade of age chances of finding a new husband are reduced. From the 50s on, there are progressively more unmarried women around than there are unmarried men. By the 70s, the ratio is totally unbalanced. Though women now live longer than men, they are still supposed to marry older men, and the pool of eligibles dries up. In spite of surgery, the cosmetics and fashion industries, and exercise, it is not possible to look youthful (read "beautiful") forever. And everyone knows that any self-respecting man is entitled to be sexually aroused over his decaffeinated breakfast coffee. So older women outlive their other primary function, that of wifing, also by their early 40s. What is left? Grandmothering? Unfortunately, surveys show that this is a peripheral role for most women. It is a consideration of what is next that is the theme of this book.

It is clear that the older woman of today has and is a problem. She is in limbo, or at least she is in transition. The models for womanhood presented by her mother and grandmother are no longer useful. She has to fumble through and make her own paths, much of the way by trial and error. By the same token, though, her daughters and granddaughters, who will be the older women of tomorrow, should have a less painful road. Unless there is a new set of social upheavals comparable to those that have led to present conditions—increased life expectancy and changed economic functioning—the older women of today will have marked trails for the older women of tomorrow.

The possibility that the conditions that exist for today's aging women may be temporary and transitional is supported by data I have gathered on generational differences in three-generation families (Troll, 1975). Less than a handful of the hundred grandmothers in the study had had any higher education; many had no formal education at all. A quarter of their daughters had had some college experience, and half of their granddaughters were either planning to attend college, were presently in college, or had graduated. Along with this shift in education are measurable generational shifts in older women's intellectual concerns, desire to achieve, traditional attitudes, and feelings of some control over their life.

Younger women have more than one perspective on the world. They see it as more complex and providing more alternative options than did their mothers. More younger women want to achieve in their own right instead of through the successes of their husbands and sons, and they believe it is possible to achieve in nontraditional, "nonfeminine" ways. Many younger women feel that they can arrange their future lives by their own efforts, that they need not wait for fate or the powers that be in the person of a Prince Charming or a fairy godmother to grant their wishes and take care of them. Today's young woman can mount her own charger and ride into battle alongside her prince! If these generational differences can be projected into the future and do not just represent age differences in the present, then some day older women will not only be trained for different kinds of lives but will also be better prepared to choose from a variety of options. They will be more insistent that they *have* options, and they will be able to shape their own lives. The generation that has espoused the woman's movement of today is likely to carry a feminist perspective into the later years of their life.

This book focuses primarily on the present generations of older women. It deals with their dilemma of transition, of trail blazing, of ignorance and uncertainty, of discovery. It presents information and guidelines that may help women broaden their perspectives and enhance their lives. It tries to describe who aging women are, what they can expect, what they deserve. Its message is that there is more to be expected from life than most older women now have and implies that there are many ways in which older women can make their lives fulfilling and worthwhile.

Eileen Foley's contribution, in the next chapter, is a very personal introduction to the real world of the older woman. In her journalistic description of three women in their 70s and 80s, Foley brings to life three very different representatives of our oldest subjects. Perhaps the most notable characteristic of these women is their vitality, their uniqueness, and their deviation from the stereotype of poor, dumb, and ugly. There is no single type of older woman, just as there is no single type of younger woman; the later years are built upon and reflect the younger years.

Our first general topic is woman's body. How much of the older woman's behavior is determined by the state of her biological being? Is it true that for a woman "biology is destiny"; that her feelings, her desires, her interests, her physical and mental health, her satisfactions are first at the mercy of her menstrual rhythms, and then destroyed when these menstrual rhythms end? The woman's movement has been challenging many of the dogmas about menstrual prepotency, but since it is primarily a young women's movement it has been less interested in attacking longstanding beliefs about menopausal prepotency. Young women do not want to look at their own aging any more than do young men. They are more interested in genital anatomy, natural childbirth, abortion, and bisexuality than in hormonal changes, waning attractiveness, and the problems of sexuality in old age. Yet many of the issues are the same. An understanding of genital anatomy should be basic information for young and old alike. Rape is a threat to young and old alike. Sexual attractiveness and finding satisfactory sex partners are central issues for both young and old. We hope that the biological information about aging presented in Part II does for older women what the many manuals and textbooks about the body in youth are doing for younger women. We want to help separate the myths from the realities, the abnormal from the normal. Unfortunately, the popular culture and the mass media, as well as many high school and college textbooks (even those used in medical schools) still circulate misinformation. Our four contributors in this area—Ruth Weg, Margaret Hellie Huyck, Carol Nowak, and Joan Israel—cover general biological changes, sexuality, the menopause, and the overwhelming importance of appearance. Both objective information and personal reactions are described to round out the picture.

Just as most people assume that the menopause makes a woman shrivel up and lose all interest in sex, they also assume that anyone over a certain age loses memory, intellectual competency, and the ability to learn anything new. When a woman thinks she is getting older, she finds herself asking such questions as: "Will my brain deteriorate?" "Will I find sex repugnant, or will it become painful, or will it become impossible?" "Will men still find me attractive?" "Do wrinkles and other signs of age turn men off?" "Will I forget who I am?" "Can old bags learn new tricks?" We have not included a chapter on intellectual changes as such but will see in later chapters that myths about decay in learning and memory parallel those about decay in health and vigor. There is more continuity in competence over many years than there is deterioration. And where there is deterioration, it may be neither irreversible nor inevitable.

It is not enough to know something about what you've got in the way of organic structure and functioning. What you feel about yourself determines or shapes what you will do with what you've got—your body and your options. Or what you feel about yourself determines what you will do about what you *haven't* got. Does personality change in the later years of life, or do people remain pretty much the same through the years? Can a person turn into a little old lady in tennis shoes if she hasn't been a little young lady in tennis shoes?

There are many ways in which people get meaning and excitement from life. Traditionally, women have found their drama in the love story and the trials and tribulations of creating and bringing up new human beings. They have been absorbed by questions like, "Will I get a man? Will he be mine forever? Will I have a boy or girl? Will my child excel at school? Will my child justify my sacrifices?"

Too often the plight of today's older woman is that she does not have the script for a new drama once the earlier ones are played out. Should she repeat the same old stories over and over? Revitalize the love of her early life or find a new knight in shining armor? Turn to grandchildren to become involved in the same crises and resolutions she experienced with her children—or follow through on the continued life dramas of her adult children? Part III of this book deals with the topic of finding meaning, fulfillment, and satisfaction in the later years. Harold Feldman's fourfold prescription for ways to life satisfaction combines old themes with new variations and provides a type of involvement suited to the variety of older women. Florine Livson raises some profound questions about continuity and discontinuity in the middle years. Helena Lopata and Sandra Candy both discuss friendship, in one case of widows and in the other of professional women. The paucity of extrafamilial resources available to most older women today is apparent in Lopata's data, while the possibilities of more enriched interpersonal relationships which Lopata projects as a consequence of changes associated with the women's movement are demonstrated as existing among women who might be considered the forerunners of today's "liberated" women, Candy's sample of teachers.

Traditionally, women's social interactions have been exclusively intimate and informal. Along with today's movement outside the home into the job world are shifts toward active participation in the informal community and civic activities and organizations previously considered the domain of men. Women who are freed of their parenting and to some extent wifing obligations move into educational endeavors, into new jobs, paid or volunteer, into clubs and formal organizations, and into politics. Bernice Neugarten, in a 1968 study, pointed out that many middle-aged women become more comfortable with their independent thoughts and assertions, and as a result make their influence felt wherever they go. In Part IV Jon Hendricks treats the usually ignored subject of leisure-time distribution. Robert Atchley and Sherry Corbett discuss jobs and retirement. Rosalyn Saltz reviews a kind of post-retirement occupational endeavor, and Nancy Schlossberg and Evaline Carsman consider the ways in which education can make life more interesting.

We have been speaking so far in a very general way, ignoring the wide group differences that exist in each area — differences between middle-class and working-class women, between rich and poor, white and black, Jewish and Irish women. The fifth section of this book points out the importance of these differences. Jacquelyne Jackson, Mildred Seltzer, Constantina Safilios-Rothschild, and Helen Fogel each describe the difference in aging in subgroups of our society. While there are undoubted variations, these seem to be, as Dr. Jackson says, more of degree than of kind. Older women in America have a lot in common.

In Part VI we address ourselves to help for older women. Psychological treatment of disturbed people has traditionally been restricted by age. Some therapists think it is not worth while to treat anybody over 12. Probably a majority of psychotherapists believe it is not worth treating anybody over 50: they believe these people are not going to change. In this book we take the position that not only is change or development possible, but where a person's life is meaningless or unlivable, therapy is desirable. A depressed person of 70 is entitled to as much help as a depressed person of 7 or 17 or 27. This position raises further professional questions. Should present-day older people who need help be treated differently from contemporary younger people? If they were brought up on such maxims as "Grin and bear it;" "Old age is no joy;" and "Don't wear your heart on your sleeve" how are they going to respond to encounter groups or even the necessary self-revelations of traditional psychotherapy? Are they going to be helped more by individual or by group treatment? When is indirect treatment better than direct? Can we anticipate the crises of psychosexual life and help people move through them? Should counseling or psychotherapy be provided as a matter of course for widows, for women undergoing mastectomy, for those given their "death sentence"? On the other hand, if we take into account the fact that the population we are talking about is comprised of the survivors, it may be that having managed to live for fifty years or more means they've learned a bag of tricks for living and surviving all sorts of crises. The treatment of older people may be much easier than the treatment of more fragile youth—a temporary helping hand may do instead of a permanent crutch. Kenneth Israel, a psychiatrist, and Elinor Waters and Betty White, group counselors, present variant ways in which older women can use help and in turn help others. Eva Kahana and Asuman Kiyak survey the larger scene of proliferating haphazard and meaningless service programs alongside the real needs of older women, particularly the oldest. They consider such particularized needs as for housing, health care, safety, money, transportation, and recreation. A woman is too often considered old on the basis of the number of years she has lived. She may still be full of life, health, and vigor. At this time, she needs to fight for equal living rights with younger women and all men. But there comes a time when even the most durable woman can no longer make it on her own. If she survives to the end, she needs the help of others—her kin, her friends—and the resources of the community. Some aging women are really old.

The theme of power and powerlessness pervades all discussions of older women's social life. In Part VII Jacqueline Goodchilds describes the tortuous path older women must travel when they are confronted with new positions of power and new ways of achieving it and, above all, displaying it. In a sense, it seems as if the present generations of older women are damned if they do and damned if they don't. Yet Robert Kastenbaum and Deborah Simonds end their discussion of charm—woman's best weapon for power through the ages—on a more optimistic note. In a way they take us forward two steps, to the point at which neither men nor women need to seek or display power in the blatant, independent way men have traditionally done and women are now finding themselves doing. But it may be possible for both men and women to benefit from the long-run effects of the women's movement by using charm—which is in a way a kind of power, in a way a method of achieving power, but also in a way a transcendence beyond power.

There are of course many topics we have not been able to deal with in this book. We have hardly done justice to the issue of intellectual functioning. We have practically ignored the places people live in—the kinds of homes and communities in which they reside—which determine the degree of their isolation or sociability, their comforts and pleasures, and their mobility and social participation. Breaking up a lifelong home and moving to new quarters can be a critical event in the life of the older woman. At best, it is a crisis of transition that sets her thinking about what has gone before and what is possible for the future. At worst, it can destroy a life fabric, cutting old threads without replacing them with new ones. Community and architectural planning for our aging population needs to consider not only internal arrangements like the design of sinks and stairs but also personal and interpersonal needs like access to transportation and congenial neighbors. Above all, we have neglected the whole sphere of women and politics—what political policies and political procedures do for women, as well as what it is like for women to be involved in the political arena.

Joan Israel, who dreamed up the idea for this book, has warned us that she already sees the need for another volume to follow.

REFERENCES

Troll, Lillian, "Generational Change in Women's Cognitive and Achievement Orientation," paper presented at Symposium on Women in the Future at International Gerontological Conference, Jerusalem, Israel, July, 1975.

Neugarten, Bernice, *Middle Age and Aging*. Chicago: University of Chicago Press, 1968.

Chapter 2

The Way It Was

Eileen Foley

To be a retired woman in 1975 is to be just under to well over 70, to have grown up in Peter Thompson middy dresses, and to have absorbed a host of catechetical definitions of "ladylike" behavior.

It is to have been badgered to speak in modulated tones, not like a fishwife, to sit with your knees together and your dress down.

It is to have grown up in an era when nice women didn't smoke or paint their faces and it is to have dared to experiment with both, redefining "niceness" in the process.

Such a woman was expected to marry a man who would be faithful to her, a good provider and a good father. In turn, she was expected to stay home, keep a clean house, and be a good mother.

But if she had a mother who worked outside the home or was active in community affairs, chances were her life paralleled her mother's.

Today's woman in retirement grew up in a less populous America, without radio, television, or telephones.

The lack of technology in their youth made many women of her era feel more self-reliant and able to evade boredom with work, reading, gardening, and creative activities.

She grew up with many more older people around her than

Eileen Foley has a Master's Degree in Social Work and has been a noted reporter on *The Detroit Press* for several years. She has written a number of articles dealing with contemporary women's issues.

youngsters do today. Her grandmother, her aunt, or her great-aunt may have lived in her house, shared her room, or even her feather bed.

"When I was a child I thought I would die at 40," said Mary, 72, a housewife. "I didn't see any advantages for myself being over 40, and I still don't. I don't think there is one redeeming feature about being old.

"I have known six generations in my family. I had a great-grandmother and I didn't like her because I thought she was so old. She was. She just sat in this rocking chair and was always trying to give me hard candy. I was a little intimidated because of her wrinkles.

"When you come down to it, I don't see why young children shouldn't be put off by old people. One of my grandsons told me it looked like I had worms under the skin in my hands, where my veins are. I can understand that."

Mary grew up in a small town in Missouri, the eldest of five children. Her parents squabbled viciously for twenty of their twenty-five years of marriage. She remembers her mother as self-directed, disciplined, and strong of character and her father as spoiled and bad-tempered.

As a teenager she had a cache of theatrical makeup which she applied on her way to high school, and, upon graduation she went to college as all her friends did. She studied journalism at Kansas State for two years, then quit for some job she says "didn't amount to much."

"I was always mad about some boy and couldn't get anywhere with him, I was so tall (nearly 6 feet), you know. It was a big handicap. I don't remember talking about getting married as a teenager, and I knew I didn't want to have children," she recalls.

"I married at 26 and didn't have children for six years. Then I had such a marvelous time with them (two sons and a daughter) I couldn't imagine being so strange about it beforehand."

There were never baby-sitters in Mary's house. Her husband came home after work and they were all together at home or wherever they went.

When the children left the nest, Mary's life grew duller. She amused herself with gardening and learning old-fashioned skills such as chair caning and upholstery. As usual, she read a lot.

There were lots of things girls didn't do when Mary grew up. "Practically everything," she said. "I think everyone my age had to put up with that, but I always accepted it. I was very repressed to say the least." Her personal expression was more subdued than her career plans.

"I never had any interest in anything except having a good time," she said. "I never got involved in the suffrage movement. Politics didn't interest me until ten years ago.

"I would vote in every election and would always ask my husband who to vote for. I didn't know the people and I couldn't care less. Then suddenly I got interested in politics. I read Richard Rovere in the New Yorker faithfully. Now Lawrence and I vote entirely differently." Fervent attitudes on behalf of any social or political causes make her uncomfortable, so she has never embraced them. Overt expressions of ambition annoy her too. "They exhaust me," she explained.

An avid reader since childhood, Mary is still involved in literature, belongs to a community book club, visits friends, works the Sunday crossword puzzle with her husband, and hopes to travel in California where a son lives and spend at least one winter in a small university town in southern France with her husband.

"I'm just falling apart generally," Mary says of her present condition. "I cannot bear it. I just resent it. You have all these aches and pains that float around. One of the worst things is seeing your friends get so old. You're so helpless to do anything about it."

The biggest change the years have wrought in her is a release from the inhibitions she grew up with. "I just do what I jolly well please and get out of things I don't want to do," she said. "I don't ever use my age as an excuse, I just say, 'no.' "

Her biggest gripe is that her doctor has forbidden her to smoke because she has emphysema, a fact she doesn't like to broadcast.

"I had been smoking for 50 years and I quit immediately. I would be sort of glad if I could smoke again," she said.

The secret to successful living as an antique is to remember to live in the present, not in the past, says Willie, who is vague about her age but says her mother died at 99 in 1973.

The mayor of Mobile was a pallbearer at her mother's funeral, says Willie, adding "I don't come from no crummy family."

"Not only can you not live in the past," Willie insists. "You can't even live from yesterday anymore."

Willie was born and raised in a middle-class black section of Mobile, one of three children of an engineer from Honduras and a fair-complexioned American Negro woman. She has a younger sister and a younger brother.

She likes the fact that the times are more open now than they were when she was coming up.

"People did a lot more sneaking around then than now. There were just as many bastards born then, too, but momma then didn't tell the kids all she was doing."

"Another difference between then and now is that then men took care of their wives. I don't know of my mother ever doing anything," she recalls nostalgically.

Reaching the point where she has to do nothing but what she chooses has made Willie's retirement, forced upon her for health reasons in 1969, the best time of her life. "There's no time clock, honey—that's the best part of it," she says.

She's annoyed by other retired women who live in her apartment building because they seem to think that being old means quitting on life and being staid.

"I came in one night after having been out drinking with friends and there was a bunch of them sitting in the lobby, just looking at me. " 'Don't worry about it,' I told them. 'I'm not going to bring disgrace on this place. I'm on the pill.' "

Willie's work life began shortly after marriage at 17, a combination her mother opposed.

"She wanted me to go to school, and she was right. I shouldn't have married that man. Marriage was not a very sweet thing with me. I made the first mistake of marrying an illiterate person. The next one was a stone drunk. He died, but it was no worry. There were no children."

She started out as a maid, cooked in a hospital kitchen, and retired as a manager of a cleaning store on Detroit's outskirts.

Being sickly takes some of the fun out of Willie's life and short money—having to live for a month on what you used to make in a week—is a hassle too.

But Willie has lots of friends and belongs to a church with a busy schedule she manages to keep up with.

"I take the bus downtown when I want to. I know what can happen to an older woman out there and I try to be alert.

"Then my friends and their friends drive me lots of places. Most of my friends are 40 and down. They are men and women, white and black, mostly white. "I don't know how I got mixed up with so many whites."

Her "best friend," Buck, is not only white but several years younger than she is.

Besides the church activities, helping to entertain people recently released from mental hospitals, and visiting friends who have had to move to nursing homes, Willie reads everything from trash to Reinhold Niebuhr, crochets, goes bar-hopping with Buck, and, once a month visits old friends who were members of a civil rights group with her in the late '60s.

"We drink wine, play cards, lie and go to the movies," she said, grinning. "Except for my health, I'm no different than I was at 20," says Willie. "Until your mind grows old, you are not old."

Willie has no regrets, though once she had hoped for children.

"Now I'm glad that I didn't have any," she says. "I might have given birth to a murderer or a dope addict."

Willie says she has never wanted for men in her life and time has not changed that. She disdains the men in her apartment building, however, describing them as "old and decrepit."

"You get propositioned all the time," she says. "There's a group of men, 25 to 50, who prefer older women. But when the men pass 50, they have some kind of idea that a woman their age ain't good for them, like Wilbur Mills, you know. They think having a younger woman will prolong their masculinity.

"But a woman is way ahead of a man, and I don't care how old she is. You remember that when you get older. You got 'de ups,' because he starts to slow down long before you do."

"I don't think of my age, ever, except when I don't want to do something. Then I become an old lady," says Beulah, 87, whose mother was a slave until just after her tenth birthday.

Beulah was born in Bradford, Pennsylvania where her father, a self-employed janitor, settled after following oil gushers west across the state. Her mother was brought to Meadville, Pennsylvania after Emancipation to work for a family there and get an education.

The work outweighed the education, and her mother went on to Brooklyn to live with relatives. Beulah has no idea how her parents met.

Beulah's mother was so eager for an education that seven years after her marriage she convinced her husband to send her away to study at an academy in upstate New York. On her return Beulah was conceived and born.

Her father died four years later at 47 and her mother took over the buildings he maintained to support herself and Beulah.

At 4 or 5 Beulah went to work with her mother, lugging waste baskets and spittoons to the back room where they were emptied and cleaned. At 9 she had an office of her own to clean before she went to school.

There was no question but that Beulah would go to high school and college. Her mother told her she would do these things, and she accepted them.

Many young black girls didn't go on to school in those days, principally because their parents didn't want them to, she believes. However, one Gertrude Curtis, a woman a few years her senior, went off to New York to study dentistry, married twice, and always kept her own name, Beulah recalls.

Beulah's mother died in 1908, before her daughter finished a two-year normal school course. Beulah dropped out of school, took a teaching job in Virginia. She returned to Bradford in 1910, married in 1911, bore her first child in 1912, left her husband and moved to Detroit in 1913. Her first job there was doing housework.

"There wasn't any marked animosity against black people, but there were just certain things you could do — cook, be a housemaid or a laundress and live with a family. No one ever heard of a Negro trying to teach."

The first job gave her $1 a day. Soon she married her second husband, a barber from Philadelphia, whom she refers to respectfully as Mr. C., and had two more children.

When World War I began, the pay for day work jumped to $3.50, she recalls, adding "I was making so much money I wasn't speaking to ordinary people."

In 1922 she began working as a social worker for the city welfare department, a job she retired from in 1953.

Like her mother before her, Beulah was active in church and community groups, beginning with organizations that served her children such as the YMCA and YWCA. Later she branched out to civil rights groups, civic groups, retired employees' groups, and the arts. Public commendations of her contributions to the community line the walls of her tiny, modern apartment.

She participated in politics even before women could vote. "I stood on the corner at election time," she recalls. "I was

Republican, and the men just worked us to death standing us out on the corner to give out literature. "When the suffrage movement came up, I was busy as anything having teas at my house, arranging teas elsewhere, going to teas, having all sorts of people come to speak, getting women in there and putting a ballot up on the wall to show them how to mark it."

Mr. C. died in 1956. In 1960 Beulah helped found a retired city employees' association in Detroit and then skipped off to Washington to direct a women's residence run by the Association of Colored Women.

For Beulah freedom to do what she chose, when she chose, didn't come with retirement. She recalls no strictures put on her as a woman. She sees new freedom with the times that affects older people as it does the young, but she worries that people haven't learned that responsibility comes with every freedom. She doesn't believe in license.

Mrs. C. says she had no ambitions to be 87. It just happened to her, much as the public acclaims that adorn her walls just happened — a result of dealing with what comes up every day.

Being 87 has its rewards, she says, mainly that "everyone raves about how pretty and beautiful I am and how smooth my complexion is. I tell them I use Lifebuoy."

"My doctor wants me to lose weight, but I think it is because my face is fat that I don't have wrinkles. I never saw a wrinkled fat face. I am not going to lose. I would lose a pound off my face before I lost one off my behind."

Since her husband's death Mrs. C. says she has moved too fast for any man to catch up with her. She calls the male senior citizens who live in her apartment building "sickening."

"I've been widowed too long and I don't have much patience. I can't think of any man I would be interested in. I don't know any men my age. They're all dead," she says. "A man 50 years old perhaps might have enough energy to be a husband, but I don't want to marry a man younger than my youngest son. I would always feel I was with one of my children. I don't want for things to do," she insists. "My date book is ridiculous."

"I am no different now than I was, except I get tired faster. I can't walk five or six blocks, but I can drive, as long as I can hold onto the wheel and see where I am going. I don't go to meetings at night any more, that's all."

"My life is no different from what it was, what it has been. People don't change. They are what they were."

PART II

The Body

Charlotte Buhler and Else Frenkel-Brunswik,* Viennese psychologists who studied hundreds of men and women in the early part of this century, traced a "biographical curve of life." The concluded that the more people derived their feelings of identity and self-worth from their physical being, the more their psychological and social aging coincided with their physical aging. Those who had other sources of meaning in life retained a youthful vitality many years after their body declined.

Nobody who survives youth keeps the body of youth, though for some it exists longer than for others. However, what effect body changes have on how we feel about ourselves is what is important. Furthermore, body changes are various and diverse. Some women run to fat, others to wrinkles, others lose energy or the use of one or another body function. But not all the decay described in "old wives' tales" and today's media needs to happen. For instance, because you stop ovulating doesn't mean you stop enjoying sex. Part II covers these and related topics.

*Else Frenkel-Brunswick. "Adjustments and Reorientations in the Course of the Life Span," in *Psychological Studies in Human Development*, eds. Raymond Kuhlen and George Thompson. (New York: Appleton-Century-Crofts, 1963).

Chapter 3

More Than Wrinkles

Ruth Weg

INTRODUCTION

Aging Is Not Disease

The idea that we can age normally is difficult for most people to accept. Aging has become identified not only with decline in body function but also with disease. This is partly the legacy of cross-sectional studies that have compared ill and institutionalized old people with college youth instead of taking a look at healthy older people. Since this medical model of aging is the one taught in medical schools, the disease mythology is perpetuated. Unfortunately, equating aging with disease inhibits the development of any predictive or preventive approach to health maintenance that could help slow down aging processes and limit debilitation from chronic diseases.

A *Newsweek* article (April 16, 1973) with the headline, "Can Aging be Cured?" reflects the image of aging as pathology. Yet longitudinal studies that follow the progress of generally healthy older people show that decrements are gradual and not as extensive as we once thought (Shock, 1974). The majority of older persons,

Ruth Weg, Ph.D., is Associate Professor of Biology and Gerontology at the Leonard Davis School of Gerontology, Andrus Gerontology Center, University of Southern California, Los Angeles. She is known internationally in the field of physiology and aging and has written widely in this area, particularly with reference to women, education for gerontology, sexuality, and physiology.

even if their functioning deteriorates in several body systems, retain ample capacities for coping with the demands of everyday living.

Rather than a disease, then, aging is a part of the developmental process from conception to death. Rather than a problem, it is a unique patterning over time, with its own characteristics, rewards, and challenges (Weg, 1976).

A Woman Is Beauty

"In Rome we say that it is the duty of every woman to be beautiful. A man is a man—it doesn't matter if he's ugly. But a woman must look as beautiful as she can, because both are happier that way." Eve of Roma, maker of cosmetics for women is pleased to use that quote in the packaging for blending creams! Eve of Roma, like so much of the beauty products industry, makes the most of the stereotypes of man and woman. The media, in general, appeal to the double standards prevalent in every stage of life. This is still a society in which youth is the yardstick, where the beauty, vigor, and performance of youth remain the ideal, the everlasting goals of adulthood, middle age, and the later years. Not only does the older woman's body change visibly with time, and her energies and achievements decline, but she suffers more acutely than the older man because these declines are added to a lifelong second-class citizenship. More than man, she must retain her youthful appearance, resorting to the creams, the makeup, and even surgery—for "she" as "youth" is the decoration of society.

From this cultural value on youth-beauty for the female of the species is born the nagging fear that life shall pass her by as she ages. She will become part of the invisible "neuter" group of older women—gray-haired, lined face and body, sagging breasts and belly, losing the battle with misplaced pounds. It is therefore, no surprise that the middle-aged and older woman feels unlovable, resigns herself to desire without gratification, becomes a prisoner of the diminished self-concept fostered by our society. It is no wonder that millions of dollars are spent each year for cosmetics, fad diets, reducing salons, exercisers, youth pills, and hairdressers.

The Diminished Image

It is true that there are real physiological age changes. For some (but not all), growing older means dry, wrinkly skin, or poorer vision and hearing, or the telltale tan and brown liver spots, or thin gray hair, or split nails, or misplaced bulges, or a slowly shrinking stature. There may also be a decrease in muscle strength and tone, reduced efficiency in cardiovascular and renal systems, achy muscles and joints, occasional breathlessness, digestive disturbances, and altered sleep patterns. Most people's taste sensitivity is dulled, as is their touch. It may take longer and require a greater expenditure of energy to complete the same task than when they were younger.

Does it follow, then, that most women have to look forward to their older years as dull, failing, painful, lonely, unlovely, and unloved? Does this mean that since the older woman can no longer maintain the picture of the young, voluptuous girl, she is no longer woman? Must she prepare for reclassification as sexless nonperson? Indeed not. For she is more than her appearance. To begin with, few women experience all of the changes described above. Even those who have one or two of them can continue a satisfactory lifestyle. A woman's greatest damage is created not by the small decreases in the efficiency of her physiology, but by her acceptance of a negative image of herself. With the approaching end of woman's procreative function, her anxieties may mount. She may worry about her appearance, her health, her intellectual capacity, the empty nest, the love of her mate, the stability of her marriage, and her future. However, there is no inevitability to physical or psychological crisis, before, during, or after menopause. Involutional melancholia is not widespread. There is no sudden disappearance of the round, full curves of the female body. Statistical morbidity and mortality data demonstrate that there are still long, healthy, vigorous years ahead (average life expectancy of 75.3 years) for a very large number of older women.

Recent experiments with diet, exercise, hormonal therapy, and involvement with life lead us to believe that part of the functional change or loss we have attributed to aging alone may be due to misuse, disuse, or disease. Dr. de Vries (1970) has demonstrated that exercise regimens can restore considerable muscle tone and strength as well as increase the sense of well-being. The confusion, disorientation, fatigue, forgetfulness, irritability, and insomnia so long ascribed to aging have been reversed by vitamins, trace nutrients, and proteins. We have mistakenly institutionalized many older persons diagnosed as organically senile who were really "pseudosenile" (e.g., Bender 1971). Moreover, the degree of change, the rate of aging is different for each of us, and different for various parts of our bodies. We are most unique and individual as we age, a blend of our inheritance and our life experiences. Because we associate decline with aging, we resign ourselves to accept the "inevitable." Until very recently, few questioned such wisdom. Let us look at the facts.

PHYSIOLOGY OF THE FEMALE BODY

Foods: Their Impact and Importance

The isolation, purposelessness, and damaged self- esteem of many older women frequently translates into a disregard for proper food intake — a marked disinterest in cooking and perhaps even subliminal intentions of self-destruction. For many older women, coffee replaces milk, toast replaces whole-grain cereal and eggs, pastries are chosen over fruits and vegetables, candies and other sweets frequently and sadly become the caresses of the later years. Nutrition may play a greater role in the appearance and physiology of older women (and men) than we thought.

Fifty or more nutrients are required for the body to provide energy and materials for all cell (and body) functions and for the synthesis of essential substances (hormones, enzymes, cell membranes, etc.). Within limits, we become what we eat. Yet during the last twenty-five years, Western cultures have significantly altered their dietary pattern away from raw fruits, vegetables, dairy products, and proteins of meat origin. Many older women (and men) have a diet too high in cholesterol and other fats, sugar, and refined grains, leading to tooth decay, atherosclerosis, obesity, diabetes, and heart disease. This "Westernized" diet also lacks bulk, and evidence is accumulating that connects this lack with the development of malignancy (Burkitt, 1973).

In recent years, considerable emphasis has been placed on the serious consequences of obesity. Dr. Ralph Nelson (1974), head of Clinical Nutrition at Mayo Clinic, blames overnutrition for reducing the life span. Large intake of refined carbohydrates ("empty calories") has been found to increase the level of serum cholesterol (adding to an increased susceptibility to cardiovascular accidents — strokes); to increase the likelihood of pancreatic exhaustion (a factor in maturity-onset diabetes); and finally to contribute to the metabolic patterns for obesity (Yudkin, 1972).

Older women in some ways may be facing a greater risk from poor nutrition than older men. Their weight increases to a maximum between the ages of 55 to 64 and the number who are obese does not drop until the late 60s or 70s (National Center for Health Statistics, Public Health Service, 1966). Even in women over 80, 20 percent have been noted to be overweight (Corless, 1973).

An increasing number of clinicians and researchers are convinced that an equal threat to optimum health in the older years may be "subclinical malnutrition" (Briggs, 1974). There are suggestions that even mild nutrient deficiency may lead to decreased learning performance, depression, confusion, and disorientation. Low vitamin and trace element intake appear to correlate with increased incidence of nervous, circulatory, and respiratory disorders. What is most important and encouraging is that corrective diet can provide amelioration of some of these disorders (Hyams, 1973).

In an effort to reduce caloric intake, frequently at the suggestion of their physicians, many older women cut down on meat, dairy products, fruits, and vegetables (Mayer, 1974), and thus do not take in enough protein, vitamins, and micronutrients for adequate maintenance of cellular function and overall health (Ten State Nutrition Survey, 1971). Protein lack may result in symptoms too familiar to many older women: edema, fatigue, malaise, and tissue wastage.

A less dramatic but fundamentally more eroding assault on the American diet, in general, comes from the large losses (from 20 to 90 percent) of micronutrients (vitamins and minerals) that result from the refining, processing, canning and overcooking of foods (Schroeder, 1970). Reduced intake of vitamins and trace elements affects a wide range of body functions since they are essential components of the enzymes that enable all cellular and general body system functioning (Bender, 1971).

Even mild malnutrition can trigger apathy and set up a circular reaction by reducing appetite, which further decreases food intake. In this way, the ability to mount an immune response to disease and the capacity for an adaptive response to stress are both lessened. Extended stress, whether emotional or physical, appears to be causally related to calcium, fatty acid, nitrogen, sodium, vitamins B and C imbalances (Scrimshaw, 1964; Hyams, 1973). Acting on each other in a circular, positive feedback, malnutrition, illness, and stress may leave the older woman unable to cope with the emotional and physical requirements of everyday living. Remember that older women (and men) need more energy to carry through any work or physiological task. Thus, they need a higher concentration of micronutrients per calorie than younger people — particularly as the caloric intake decreases and stress increases.

Diet has been found to be related to the age at which women die. Those whose diets were rich in ascorbic acid, low in fat, and high in protein lived longer (Chope, 1954). Unfortunately, few older women can be said to eat properly. In a study at Michigan State University, 95 percent of 97 white and 104 black women (between the ages of 40 and 80) had nutrient intake below 80 percent of the recommended dietary allowance (Kelley et al., 1975).

While we cannot assume that a "good" diet will cure disease or prolong life, we can suggest that a balanced diet fashioned to the individual needs of the older woman is essential to even moderate emotional and physical health. This balanced diet would help retain a higher level of appropriate function, and modulate the rate of aging. Furthermore, eating is not only nutrient intake, but also a social event, a symbol of affection and concern from other human beings.

Exercise: Slimming Down, Firming Up

In the last few years, older women (and men) have developed a "physically fit" conscience. A sensible, regular exercise regimen can lead to better appearance and functioning. According to Butler and Lewis (1976), "physical fitness is a quality of life, a condition of looking and feeling well, having necessary physical reserves to enjoy a range of interests, among which is sex." Dynamic fitness describes a person free of disease but also able to move vigorously and energetically, improving the "efficiency of heart and lungs, muscular strength and endurance, balance, flexibility, coordination and agility."

Exercise will strengthen and improve muscle tone in the arms, legs, stomach, back, chest and neck. It can stimulate bone synthesis and prevent calcium loss from bones. Exercise and good nutrition are interventions well within the reach of most older women and invaluable in fighting "droop" and "flab."

Ptosis or "dropping" of the pelvic viscera is a fairly frequent complaint of the older woman (particularly if she has given birth to many children). If uncorrected, incontinence may become a major nuisance. The Kegel (Lanson, 1975) exercises, designed for the female body, can improve the muscle tone of the vaginal wall as well as other pelvic structures—uterus, bladder, urethra, and rectum. With continued application, incontinence is minimized, and sexual interest and behavior may be enhanced.

The sluggishness that is a common partner of the inactive older woman may, in turn, lead to depressed appetite, weariness, an increased incidence of illness, and a decrease of adaptive behavior. It has been recognized that for young and old alike, physical activity is conducive to feelings of well-being, self-confidence, motivation, renewed sexual interest, and a vital appearance.

Insult and Injury

ORAL HEALTH. The periodontal disease and accompanying loss of teeth that for so long were considered a "mark" of aging is preventable. Oral dysfunction lowers an already fragile self-image, and can be compounded by a decline in nutritional status. Some women (and men) may have a predisposition to periodontal disease. This disease of tooth-supporting structures (gum and bone tissue) may lead to eventual loosening and loss of the teeth. There are sufficient studies to suggest that dental care and balanced nutrition may act to retard, even prevent toothless faces or full dentures.

CIGARETTE SMOKING. Smoking is clearly related to disease and death (Bierman and Hazzard, 1973) in the form of lung and mouth cancer and pulmonary and cardiovascular diseases. Yet the rate of women smokers has increased more rapidly than men in the last two decades. A recent report noted that even wrinkles around the eyes are deeper for smokers.

HYPERTENSION. Those women who have juggled their lives to combine homemaking and working appear to be among those developing hypertension and cardiovascular disease at a steeper rate than those who are homemakers alone (Benjamin, 1974).

STRESS. One of the marked differences in our bodies between the early and later years is the greater difficulty with maintenance of homeostasis. For example, resting heart rate, blood pressure, and body temperature may be measured before exercise and immediately after, at one, one and one-half, and two minutes. In an older woman (and man), it takes longer for those values to return to the "pretest" level after any kind of stimulus, physical or emotional.

Stress has been implicated as a predisposing factor in atherosclerosis, coronary heart disease, and hypertension. Any change in life pattern may contribute to faster age changes and illness among older women (and men). There is a 75 percent correspondence between the number of life changes measured by the Social Readjustment Rating Scale and illness during the year following (Rahe et al., 1970). And older women in this country face many profound changes: loss of spouse and friends, of familial "mother" and "wife" roles, move to another abode, lowered standard of living, and waning community status. Stress leads to increase in adrenaline, noradrenaline, and corticosteroids. Sustained unresolved stress, and therefore long-term elevation of these hormones, will have generalized metabolic effects in addition to possible toxic effects on heart muscle, blood vessels, and ionic balance. Those peoples in the world who live exceptionally long generally have a lifestyle devoid of the kind of stress that is part of the American scene.

OSTEOPOROSIS. This disorder is found in almost a third of the people over 65 and is four times more common in women than in men. It is a painful disease and results in a loss of total bone mass—observable in loss of height, difficulty in maintaining normal posture, fragile bones, and frequent acute pain. At one time it was considered only a postmenopausal pathology and primarily estrogen-dependent. However, treatment with estrogen has benefited some people but not others (Bartter, 1973). Increased dietary calcium has stimulated protein retention and activation of osteoblasts, which results in the net synthesis of bone. Lifetime dietary habits and genetic factors for dense bones may be more significant than estrogen in maintenance of good bone structure.

ARTHRITIS. There is little doubt that large numbers of older women suffer with some degree of joint disease. It affects 14 percent of men but 23 percent of women beyond 45. The cause is still vague. Some researchers claim joint diseases are autoimmune reactions of the aging body involving destruction of healthy tissues; others identify the family of arthritic disorders as a result of delayed activity of occult viruses. A number of drugs can relieve symptoms and pain and prolong relatively normal mobility.

The Reality of the Older Female Body:
Procreation and Recreation

Almost every human being begins *in utero* with all of the natural biological equipment for reproduction and sexual interactions. The sex hormones (in the female, estrogen and progesterone) are responsible for the stimulation of sexual attraction and activity, for the differentiation and growth of the reproductive function and structure from conception through old age. These hormones also influence developmental processes beyond reproduction including cardiovascular function, development of bone and muscle, salt and water balance, and probably immunity to disease.

After about 70 years of age, continued sex steroid (hormonal) starvation results in gradual atrophy of the uterus and vagina and involution of related genital tissue. The elasticity of the skin decreases, glandular tissues diminish, and there is a loss of muscle tone which leads to relaxation of ligaments. Therefore breast and other area contours are less firm and round.

Some vulvar tissue is lost, the mons flattens, and the major labia are also less full. The minor labial covering (or hood) decreases along with the mons fatty tissue. Although there may be a modest reduction in the size of the clitoris, "there is no objective evidence to date to suggest any appreciable loss in sensate focus" (Masters and Johnson, 1974, pp. 337, 338). Appropriate stimulation results in clitoral excitation and probable orgasm. Vaginal mucosa becomes thinner, decreases in length and the earlier rugal pattern is smoother. Glands that lubricate the vagina may also be fewer in number. Vaginitis may become more frequent. Cervix, uterus, and ovaries grow smaller and may approximate prepubertal size. Portions of the urinary tract, the urethra and bladder, frequently undergo similar changes.

REPRODUCTIVE DECLINE IN THE LATER YEARS. While many older women resolve their conflicts about body changes positively, there is one area of function in which any decline is difficult to accept. One organ system — the reproductive system — stands out in special relief, apart from all others. There are few changes with age that appear to be as threatening to ego, identity, and sense of well-being as changes in one's sexuality. Reproductive decline suggests an end to active life, and an end to sexual expression. Our culture still equates youthful sexual performance with manliness or womanliness. Any loss or dysfunction is therefore interpreted as a step closer to asexuality, soon followed by death.

The view that sexual activity is the essence of life—especially long-life—is an old, familiar theme in the history of thought. Through prehistory to modern times, the human family has been preoccupied with rejuvenation. Even now, in post-industrialized societies, the measure of youth and potential for immortality is sexual capacity and performance (Trimmer, 1970). Powerful tools that have been used in the drive for a more vigorous, longer life are prayer, magic, and sorcery. Potions, folklore medicants, plant and animal tissue derivatives have places in the eternal search for youth (sexuality) and everlasting life. Gerovital, a modern-day elixir, is claimed by Aslan (1974) as a panacea for countless dysfunctions or diseases and as a deterrent to aging. Other contemporary remedies, drugs, special foods, and even a few medical practices are still used by some to hold off old age a little longer. So far, no magic formula has been proved.

Sexuality is a part of the whole person. Expression of sexuality at any age is a function of prenatal development and postnatal experiences building from a definite, inherent sexuality. Because growth and development are different for each of us, human sexuality is flexible and covers a wide range of behavior. Procreation is a necessity for the human race. But human sexuality is more than procreation and genitalia, more than orgasm, and more than sex hormones. It suggests the capacity for involvement in all of life that relates to the fact of two sexes. Sexual differentiation is the enabling factor in man-woman relationships and family structure (Weg, 1975).

As with other needs of people, the need for expression of sensuality and sexuality continues throughout life, into the ninth and tenth decades. The human need for intimacy, love, identity, and human interchange is crucial. The intimacies and warmth associated with human sexuality have importance greater than the release of sexual tension. A total personality is the participant in sexual behavior, not just anatomy and physiology. When viewed as "an isolated human function," as technique and learned ritual, "sex becomes a meaningless aside," depersonalized and mechanical (May, 1969). As an affirmation of connection to the energy of life, it is a meaningful assertion and commitment of self.

Older persons are the "sexual rejects" of our society. They are described as sexually disinterested and inert. This is particularly true of the older women. "That old women are repulsive is one of the most profound esthetic and erotic feelings in our culture" (Sontag, 1972). Young people are often anxious and embarrassed by the notion that older people (particularly their parents) still reach out for intimacy, pleasure, and tenderness in sexual expression. It is generally believed that desire diminishes, or even disappears, with age. Or that, should desire and interest remain, there may be danger in lovemaking because of the frailties of age. The image of an older woman's body in a loving embrace with the firm, vital body of a young man is repulsive to many. A psychoanalyst would view the youth in such a couple as a victim of an Oedipal complex, and such a union as a break with a powerful taboo.

Woman's developmental cycle is complete as she moves from "young and sexy" to "mature and exciting" — and finally, after 50, into the anonymity of the sexually unseen (Butler and Lewis, 1973). Her older body is deemed unattractive, undesirable. The impact of these attitudes on the woman in the middle and older years is recognized in the acting out of a self-fulfilling prophecy. The stamp of youth fades, the self-image falters, and doubts appear about adequacy as a sexual partner. Such attitudes on the part of an older woman may damage integrated, loving behavior.

INTEREST AND CAPACITY. There is now considerable documentation that sexual interest and activity exist into the ninth decade and beyond (Kinsey, 1953; Masters and Johnson, 1966, 1970; Pfeiffer and Davis, 1972). Although decline in sexual expression does occur, it has been found to be due to illness of one or both partners, not a function of age alone.

The older woman is particularly advantaged since "there is no time limit drawn by advancing years to female sexuality" (Masters and Johnson, 1966, p. 247). But she is also disadvantaged. Interest and capacity remain relatively high, but lack of opportunity and her early stereotyped sex education frustrate healthy involvement. Even the older woman herself sees lovemaking as a prerogative of the young. The morality of her growing-up years declared procreation as the primary sexual goal. Cessation of sexual relationship among older persons was reported by 14 percent of males and 40 percent of the females over 65. This difference between older men and women is only apparent, because in this age group marital coitus is typically initiated by a man's desire. It is man's reduced desire and functioning, rather than woman's loss of interest and capacity, that makes the difference. Some older women withdraw from sexual activity and even express revulsion about sexuality as a protection against the aloneness of widowhood and the coolness of a mate's ardor. Further, many older women are forced to put sexual activity at a low priority because of the "double standard of aging" still with us. Age is not a barrier for the "mature, attractive older man," but it is for the older woman. Older men seek a variety of outlets for sexual expression, without guilt and with societal approval. Older women are generally not so free.

A comparison of sexual interest between the younger and the older years highlights the constancy of sexual drives throughout life. Earlier interest, enjoyment, and frequency determine the nature of sexual interactions in later life.

CLIMACTERIC OR CHANGE OF LIFE. The older woman has lived through the years of climacteric, a period that begins as reduced fertility and lowered likelihood of pregnancy. Fewer follicles in the ovary respond to the stimulation of pituitary hormones accompanied by irregular or absent menses. Upon follicle exhaustion the primary estrogen source is gone and may lead progressively to loss of support to vascular and genital tissues. Estrogen and progesterone (female sex hormones) concentration and activity decrease in proportion to the slow atrophy of the ovarian tissue. The lowered amount of estrogen is often insufficient to stimulate the uterine lining to a former premenstrual condition. Some women do describe a common transitory discomfort—the "hot flash." Sweaty and red patches on the chest, neck, and face are the visible marks of the generated heat.

During the two to three years of irregular menses before menopause (cessation of menstruation), there may be some irregular bleeding. If the bleeding is excessive and troublesome, it is easily correctable by dilation and curettage (D&C). Statistics indicate that malignancy may be involved in less than one-fourth of postmenopausal bleeding. Approximately three-fourths of all such bleeding will gradually stop without medical or surgical intervention (Procope, 1971), but there should be medical supervision for the correction of other benign conditions that may be involved. Secondary sex characteristics and other metabolic processes (protein synthesis, bone formation, salt and water balance, reciprocal hormonal interaction) are maintained at a newly established homeostatic level for some time to come.

Many marriage manuals and gynecological texts still note other symptomatology during this period: palpitation, irritability, anxiety, depression, loss of appetite, insomnia, and headaches (Scully and Bart, 1975). Research findings, however, show that these complaints involve so few women that they may not be considered "characteristic." Secondly, when these symptoms do exist, they are more frequently a result of psychosocial factors related to being an older woman in our society rather than to changing physiology. In fact, the majority of middle-aged and older women are aware of "the change" only because their menstrual periods are fewer and farther between.

AS SEXUAL PARTNERS. The older woman need experience little sexual difficulty. A positive attitude toward sexuality, moderate good health and an available, effective partner can extend sexual activity until the very late years.

With increasing age, a decrease in the rate of neuronal responsivity and hormonal (steroid) starvation combine to create the already noted anatomical changes, and may, in some older women, present temporary difficulties for function as sexual partners. Under hormonal deprivation, thinning vaginal walls combined with decreased lubrication may cause cracking and bleeding, and penetration becomes uncomfortable for both partners. Uterine contractions during orgasm may be painful. Bladder and urethra may also be undergoing some atrophy (shrinking), and become more vulnerable to irritation. Intercourse may cause burning and frequent urination.

Intensity of physiological response and duration of anatomical and functional reactions to effective stimulation are reduced in all four phases of the sexual response cycle (Masters and Johnson, 1966, 1970).

1. *Excitement phase.* It may take as much as five minutes to lubricate sufficiently (in younger years 15 to 30 seconds may have been sufficient). This delay is comparable to the situation of the older male, in whom erective delay is also a natural fact of the older years. Vaginal expansion is reduced in reaction time and extent. Vasocongestion, purple in the younger years appears pink in the older woman.

2. *Plateau phase.* A deep skin coloration of the minor labia, predictive of imminent orgasm, is absent. The major labia may hang limply in folds around the vaginal opening. However, the clitoral response is similar in every way to that of the younger woman.

3. *Orgasmic phase.* There is a gradual reduction in the duration of orgasm between 50 to 70 years. Uterine contractions may be spastic and fewer. Vaginal contractions are also diminished.

4. *Resolution phase.* A more rapid resolution (as with older men) is related to female sex steroid imbalance. The moderately expanded vagina, elevated uterus, and other pelvic viscera relax quickly to the prestimulatory state. What faint color did develop in the minor labia begins to fade even before orgasm is complete.

The above, normal aging aspects of female functional genitalia do not all appear in all women at the same time of their lives. Withal, there can be heightened arousability and interest (Kinsey, 1953; Masters and Johnson, 1966, 1970). Menopausal and postmenopausal women can maintain the multiorgasmic capacity of their earlier years (Roszak, 1969; Lanson, 1975). The androgens continue to be secreted in amounts now relatively greater than the diminished estrogens. The decrease in female hormones is no signal for sexual inadequacy. A portion of sex steroid inadequacy or starvation can be overcome in most women with regular sexual stimulation and activity. Even surgical removal of ovaries and/or uterus (hysterectomy) has little physiological consequence. Self-image and other affective factors appear to be more important. Women who have given their lives to mothering and homemaking do not accommodate to the body changes easily. Those who chose to combine the traditional roles of homemaker-mother-wife with a worker role outside the home appear more free from those physical and psychological changes touted as being inevitable and widespread (Neugarten, 1968; Gorney and Cox, 1973).

DYSFUNCTION. What contributes to the myth of impotence and sexlessness after 65? The factors are not so different from those that affect sexual expression at any age: systemic diseases, pathology and surgery of the urogenital system, emotional health, and societal attitudes. Anemia, diabetes, fatigue, malnutrition, obesity, and a variety of metabolic abnormalities at any life stage, if untreated, may interfere with desire, abort arousal and sexual climax, and generally spoil the quality of life.

For a variety of reasons, the older woman has more of these symptoms than the younger woman. Her fear that sexual involvement may aggravate an illness, or possibly cause death (Masters and Johnson, 1970) plays a major inhibiting role. The facts belie this fear. Increases in heart rate, blood presure, oxygen consumption, and energy expenditure involved in sexual activity are moderate, comparable to walking up a flight of stairs. There is only an estimated 1 percent sudden coronary death during or after intercourse and only extreme coronary pathology calls for abstiner.ce. Rather than being a threat to health, the increase in corticosteroids and the moderate increase in cardiovascular function stimulated by intercourse create a sense of well-being, may temper arthritic pain, and can minimize physical and emotional tensions (Butler and Lewis, 1973).

"It is a myth that once you become terminally ill, you no longer have any sex desire. The drive and capability can still be there." So said an associate professor at the graduate school of social work at the University of Pittsburgh (Jaffe, 1976). Diagnosed as having leukemia in April 1973, Mrs. Jaffe discussed the role of sexuality at a recent symposium at the Foundation of Thanatology in New York City. She emphasized that "in the terminally ill, sex desire may actually increase to counter the anxiety" over dying.

Chronic diseases may have secondary physiological effects on the reproductive system and sexual expression. Overeating, often a substitute for the emptiness of living, is damaging to self-image, and may lead to other serious consequences in metabolism and cardiovascular health. Despite continued libido, there is reported difficulty in vaginal lubrication in diabetic women. A number of drugs may impair or completely depress sexual arousal and capacity. Typical geriatric medical practice has made excessive use of drugs that tranquilize and mask legitimate physical complaints of older women (and men).

The most direct effects stem from dysfunction or surgery of the urogenital system. Although clinical data suggest that hysterectomies depress desire and interfere with capacity for climax in some women, these effects are not necessary consequences (Post, 1967). Some who have had low sex energy all their lives may use a hysterectomy as a legitimate excuse for stopping sexual activity. Fear of inadequacy may be more important than any surgical aftermath.

ESTROGEN THERAPY. Estrogen deficiencies are responsive to

treatment which can minimize discomfort and genital changes. Masters (1974) has stated that "the disinclination of the medical and behavioral professions to treat the aging population for sexual dysfunction has been a major disservice perpetrated by those professions upon the general problem."

Estrogen replacement therapy does not delay the onset of menopause, and does not keep the older woman "forever young." However, there are significant effects. Estrogen can "revitalize atrophic vaginal and vulvar tissues in the older woman" (Lanson, 1975). Vaginal tissue becomes thicker and more elastic again; synthesis of fatty tissue around labial folds increases again, forming a protection for the sensitive clitoris; the blood supply improves; vaginal lubrication is more readily achieved—all contribute to a potentially more satisfying sexual response. It is generally true that for many women, estrogen replacement helps the appearance of the hair; and the skin and breasts become more firm.

Estrogen is also considered by some clinicians and researchers to play a protective role in the prevention or limitation of coronary disease, stroke, arteriosclerosis/atherosclerosis, and osteroporosis. Dosage needs to be individual and prescribed with care by a clinician, since some women react to estrogen replacement with one or more of these symptoms: stomach upset, swollen breasts and ovaries, elevated blood pressure, and weight gain as a result of fluid retention.

Some gynecologists and researchers are of the opinion that the emotional and physiological changes that accompany women's middle and old age deserve hormonal (estrogen and progesterone) or estrogen replacement as an alternative to the widespread use of sedation and/or psychotherapy (Masters and Johnson, 1970; Schleyer-Saunders, 1971). The skeletal, genital, and muscular tissue changes are not modified by sedatives. Psychotherapy is useful in the treatment or even the avoidance of depression, but has no measurable effect on metabolism.

There is no agreement about the increased susceptibility to cancer of menopausal women on estrogen replacement. In a two-year study of estrogen replacement therapy on 1,200 postmenopausal women, there was no laboratory or clinical evidence that the treatment caused cancer (Rhoades, 1974). It is noteworthy that 90 percent of uterine cancers are in women over age 40; the likelihood of breast cancer also increases with age—in both situations estrogen stores are low (Leis, 1967). Dr. Robert

Keitner of Harvard Medical School is of the opinion that any danger is attributable to too much of the hormone (quoted in *Newsweek*, December 8, 1975, p. 93).

However, there are other clinicians, such as Dr. Paul Morrow of Los Angeles County–USC Medical Center, who are convinced that the risk is too great. "The benefits are to improve the comfort and well-being of the patient, but estrogen may not be a benefit to her health" (quoted in *Newsweek*, December 8, 1975, p. 93). Late in 1975, studies supported by the Food and Drug Administration suggest that "conjugated estrogens have an etiologic role in endometrial carcinoma" (Ziel and Finkle, 1975). According to four recent studies (FDA Drug Bulletin, February-March, 1976), epidemiologic data have been developed that make a persuasive argument for increased risk in endometrial cancer with extended use of conjugated estrogens by postmenopausal women. There would appear to be cause for caution, awaiting further studies and information essential before a definitive position can reasonably be taken on estrogen therapy. Studies that would test the efficacy of estrogen and progesterone replacement therapy rather than estrogen replacement alone are necessary, particularly in view of the differential role of these hormones and the suggestive carcinogenic implications.

SEX THERAPY.   There are presently large numbers of sex counselors across the country, but relatively few can be considered therapists for older men and women. Dr. Ann Sviland (1975) of Los Angeles is convinced that older persons are responsive to sexual counseling. In her work, she has been able to help many older couples regain satisfying, active sexual lives. Dr. Sviland treats the whole relationship, so that communication, intimacy, and self-esteem grow measurably along with enhanced sexual capacity. This is a reminder that sexuality is more than orgasm—technique alone doesn't make a mutually pleasurable relationship.

NOT BY BODY ALONE:
THE HUMAN DIMENSION

The Present

This culture has defined woman's role as largely procreational, and has given societal approval and rewards to her for the provision of emotional, physical, and psychological support to children, husband, and home. It is no accident, therefore, that the late middle-aged and older woman who has accepted this niche becomes overwhelmed with doubt. This primary role at an end, beauty pales, and such women feel undone by the years, with few ties to a societal place.

If she chooses, a woman has qualities to nurture beyond the body beautiful: sense of self-dignity, the capacity to learn, to be challenged, to be involved in the mainstream of the society. The effort to maintain and develop the whole person all through the life span—intellectually, emotionally, and physically—provides the opportunity to enjoy the process and plan for the future.

Although the older woman experiences various degrees of physiological decline, these decrements do not signal the withering of the person. With only moderate attention to what is possible in nutrition, exercise, and adequate time for rest and relaxation, a functional, responsive physiology is probable.

Relative good health provides the energy and motivation to pursue an active lifestyle, to insure against the purposelessness of the 65 + years, and for continued growth as a total personality.

The Future

Women (in the middle of 1975) made up 13.2 million of the 22.7 million persons over 65 — about 144 older women to 100 men. By the year 2000, that ratio may be about 154 to 100, in an older population of approximately 30.6 million.

Imagine a world in which more and more of the biomedical studies in aging and health maintenance are successful. Should multiphasic medical screening be adopted, should predictive and preventive medicine become a part of the morality of society, the older woman will be freed of the debilitating chronic diseases we now associate with the later years. She will remain even more vigorous and vital.

The changing roles of men and women in the society, albeit moving slowly, suggest that the older woman of the future may be significantly different. She may achieve a satisfying combination of worker, wife, and mother roles; she may be healthier, better educated, live longer, and develop a life-span perspective. She may no longer define her existence primarily in terms of "the man" and "the children" in her life. She may choose, without penalty, to remain unmarried or share the years with another woman. A woman may be able to go beyond the single-dimensioned looking-glass image, beyond superficial attractiveness, to the whole person.

REFERENCES

Aslan, A., "Theoretical and Practical Aspects of Chemotherapeutic Techniques in the Retardation of the Aging Process," in *Theoretical Aspects of Aging*, ed. M. Rockstein, M. Sussman, and J. Chesky, pp. 45-156. New York: Academic Press, 1974.

Bartter, F. C., "Bone as a Target Organ: Toward a Better Definition of Osteoporosis," *Perspectives in Biology and Medicine*, 16 (1973), 215-31.

Bender, A. E., "Nutrition of the Elderly," *Royal Society of Health Journal* (England), 91, No. 3 (May-June 1971), 115-21.

Benjamin, B., "Mortality Trends in Europe," *World Health Statistics Report* 27, No. 1 (1974).

Bierman, E. L., and W. R. Hazzard, "Old Age, Including Death and Dying," in *Biologic Ages of Man From Conception Through Old Age*, ed. E. W. Smith, and E. L. Bierman, Chap. 10. Philadelphia: W. B. Saunders, 1973.

Briggs, G., quotes from a newspaper report of comments at the Fourth Annual Nutrition Conference of the Dairy Council of California. *Los Angeles Times*, April 25, 1974.

Brotman, H., *Every Tenth American*, Report to the Special Committee on Aging, U.S. Senate, 1975.

Burkitt; D., "Diverticular Disease of the Colon, Epidemiologic Evidence Relating it to Fiber Depleted Diets," *Transactions of Medical Society of London*, 89 (1973), 81-84.

Butler, R. N., and M. I. Lewis, *Aging and Mental Health: Positive Psychosocial Approaches*. St. Louis: C. V. Mosby Co., 1973.

———, *Sex After Sixty*. New York: Harper & Row, 1976.

Can aging be cured? *Newsweek*, April 16, 1973, pp. 56-66.

Chope, H. D., "Relation of Nutrition to Health in Aging Persons," *California Medicine*, 81 (1954), 335-38.

Corless, D., "Diet in the Elderly," *British Medical Journal*, 4, No. 885 (October 20, 1973), 158-60.

deVries, H. A., "Physiological Effects of an Exercise Training Regimen upon Men Aged 52-88," *Journal of Gerontology*, 25, No. 4 (October 1970), 325-36.

_____, *Vigor Regained: A Simple, Proven, Home Program for Restoring Fitness and Vitality*. Englewood Cliffs, N.J.: Prentice-Hall, 1974.

Gorney, S., and C. Cox, *After Forty: How Women Can Achieve Fullfillment*. New York: Dial Press, 1973.

Hyams, D. E., "Nutrition of the Elderly", *Modern Geriatrics*, 3, No. 7 (1973), 352-59.

Jaffe, reported in *Los Angeles Times*, March 21, 1976, Part I, p. 8.

Kelley, L., M. A. Ohlson, and L. V. Harper, "Food Selection and Well-Being in Aging Women," *Journal of American Dietetic Association*, 33 (1957), 466.

Kinsey, A. C., W. B. Pomeroy, C. J. Martin, and O. H. Gebhard, *Sexual Behavior in the Human Female*. Philadelphia: W. B. Saunders, 1953.

Lanson, L., *From Woman to Woman: A Gynecologist Answers Questions About You and Your Body*. New York: Alfred A. Knopf, 1975.

Leis, H., reported in *Medical World News*, 8 (1967), 63.

Masters, W. H., and V. E. Johnson, *Human Sexual Inadequacy*, pp. 337-38. Boston: Little, Brown, 1970.

_____, *Human Sexual Response*. Boston: Little, Brown, 1966.

Masters, W. H., from remarks at a lawyers' wives meeting in Beverly Hills, May 3, 1974.

May, R., *Love and Will*. New York: W. W. Norton & Co., 1969.

Mayer, J., "Aging and Nutrition," *Geriatrics*, 29, No. 5 (May 1974), 57-59.

Nelson, R. A., quotes from newspaper report of comments at the 4th Annual Nutrition Conference of the Dairy Council of California, *Los Angeles Times*, April 25, 1974, Part VI, pp. 1, 8.

Neugarten, Bernice L., ed., *Middle Age and Aging: A Reader in Social Psychology*. Chicago: University of Chicago Press, 1968.

Pfeiffer, E., and G. Davis, "Determinants of Sexual Behavior in the Elderly," *Journal of the American Geriatrics Society*, 20, No. 4 (1972), 151-58.

Post, F., "Sex and Its Problems," *Practitioner*, 199 (1967), 377-82.

Procope, B., "Aetiology of Postmenopausal Bleeding," *Acta Obstetrica et Gynecologica Scandinavica*, 50 (1971), 311-13.

Rahe, H., J. Mahan, Jr., and R. J. Arthur, "Prediction of Near Future Health Change from Subjects Preceding Life Changes," *Journal of Psychosomatic Research*, 14 (1970), 401-106.

Rhoades, F. P., "Continuous Cyclic Hormonal Therapy," *Journal of the American Geriatrics Society*, 22, No. 4 (April 1974), 183-85.

Roszak, R., "The Human Continuum," in *Masculine/Feminine: Readings in Sexual Mythology and the Liberation of Women*, p. 305. New York: Harper & Row, 1969.

Schleyer-Saunders, E., "Results of Hormone Implants in Treatment of the Climacteric," *Journal of the American Geriatric Society*, 19, No. 2 (1971), 114-21.

Schroeder, H. A., "Environment and the Quality of Life," *Saturday Review*, October 3, 1970, pp. 53, 54.

Scrimshaw, N. S., "Nutrition and Stress," in *Diet and Bodily Constitution*, ed. G. E. W. Wolstenholme and M. O'Connor, pp. 40-54. Boston: Ciba Foundation Study Group, #17, 1964.

Scully, D., and P. Bart, "A Funny Thing Happened On the Way to the Orifice: Women in Gynecology Textbooks," *American Journal of Sociology*, 78, No. 4 (1973), 1045-50.

Shock, Nathan W., "Physiological Theories of Aging," in *Theoretical Aspects of Aging*, ed. M. Rockstein, M. Sussman, and J. Chesky. New York: Academic Press, 1974.

Sontag, S., "The Double Standard of Aging," *Saturday Review*, September 1972, pp. 29-38.

Sviland, A., "Helping Elderly Couples Become Sexually Liberated: Psychosocial Issues," *The Counseling Psychologist*, 5, No. 1 (1975).

Ten State Nutrition Survey, 1968-1971 (Highlights) DHEW Publication (No. HSM 72-8134).

Trimmer, E., *Rejuvenation*. New York: A. S. Barnes & Co., 1970.

Weg, R. B., "Physiology and Sexuality in Aging," in *Sexuality and Aging* ed. I. M., Burnside. Los Angeles: Andrus Gerontology Center, 1975.

———, "The Changing Physiology of Aging," in *Aging: Prospects and Issues*, ed. R. H. Davis. Los Angeles: Andrus Gerontology Center, 1976.

Yudkin, J., "Sugar and Disease," *Nature*, 239, No. 5369 (September 22, 1972), 197-99.

Ziel, H. K., and W. D. Finkle, "Increased Risk of Endometrical Carcinoma Among Users of Conjugated Estrogens," *New England Journal of Medicine*, 293, No. 23 (1975), 1167-70.

Chapter 4

Sex and the Older Woman

Margaret Hellie Huyck

How does aging affect the way we experience sexuality? Does time dim a woman's charms? Does passion persist? Can only a "Baby" light his fire? Who kindles the flame in the mature woman? Is ripeness all?

"Sexuality" remains an important part of functioning throughout life. It includes behaviors related to genital arousal and orgasmic release. These are traditionally assessed by measures of heterosexual intercourse, orgasmic response, masturbation frequency, oral-genital activity, and sometimes by incidence of various "pre-intercourse" activities such as kissing and fondling. "Sexuality" also includes more general actions which serve to affirm the sense of self as feminine (or masculine). For example, sexuality in this sense may be reflected in styles of dress and of personal interaction. It is part of the psychic economy of the individual and can be important in maintaining positive self-feelings and in helping to adapt to change.

So far, there has been little research on sexuality among older women. Some of the reasons for this neglect are related to age and some to gender. There are several reasons why nobody has thought to study sexuality among any old people. For one, we still have a

Margaret Hellie Huyck is Associate Professor of Psychology at the Illinois Institute of Technology. One of her major research interests is sex differences in aging. She is the author of *Growing Older*, a book about the general problems of aging.

taboo against sex in old age. As Pfeiffer and Davis (1972) have suggested, this is probably more than a hangover from the Victorian era. It persists with such remarkable tenacity that present-day processes must be helping to maintain the taboo (Pfeiffer, Verwoerdt, and Wang, 1968). We still believe that sexual activity is primarily intended for procreation, and that its recreational function is secondary. Since in old age it is no longer possible to maintain the illusion that sex is carried on for reproductive purposes, it cannot be "morally" condoned. Another possible reason for the strength of the taboo may be an extension of the incest taboo. Who wants to think about one's old mother "doing it"? Therefore, who would want to research it? Also, Pfeiffer notes, the current ruling generation can try to eliminate the aged as competitors for sexual objects by stereotyping them as asexual.

Some additional factors operate particularly against research on female sexuality. For one, women have long been assumed to be sexual only with respect to men. Their sexuality was a problem when their male partners were dissatisfied with their performance, not when their own sexual needs were unmet. For example, men might be considered to need sexual activity to ensure good health, but not women. Since many older women do not have husbands, the norms for their behavior are not clear at all. As Gebhard (1971) has pointed out,

> After proselytizing for sex among the married and stressing its intrinsic value, society cannot abruptly reverse its stand again when a death or divorce renders a person unmarried. On the other hand, society cannot discard conventional morality, which demands coitus be confined to those married to one another. The escape from this dilemma is the usual one: ignore and minimize the problem as much as possible, but if you are forced to take a position then condemn publicly and condone privately. . . . As a result of this socially useful hypocrisy, the previously married are allowed greater freedom than those who never married (p. 58).

It is difficult to generalize about sexuality in older women because women differ from each other in many ways that affect their sexuality. One obvious variable is social class, as documented by Kinsey and his associates (1953). In general, women with more education and higher occupational status tend to be more experimental in their sexual practices, to enjoy it more, and to experience more orgasms than women in lower social classes. Bernard points out that the pretty woman, for all intents and purposes, is of a different sex from the homely one. "She has more privileges and prerogatives; her relations with men are of a different order" (Bernard, 1972, p. 14). Even within age and social class groups, female sexuality patterns are highly variable, apparently more so than male patterns. For this reason, any general statements about women's sexuality are less reliable than those about men's (Kaplan, 1974a, p. 109).

Age is an important factor. In the first place, age is related to maturational and biological changes, and some of these affect sexuality. Secondly, older women have experienced more of life than younger women. Most importantly, the women who are now old experienced, as girls and young women, different cultural expectations about sexual behavior from those presented to young women today. Many generational differences relate more to historical shifts in values and practices than to any intrinsic developmental processes. We will explore age differences and age changes more fully.

Keeping the limitations of existing data in mind, it appears that women in the middle years (roughly 35 to 60) are more responsive and more orgasmic than younger women, but find it increasingly difficult to find adequate satisfaction in marital intercourse (Kinsey et al., 1953; Masters and Johnson, 1970; Bell and Lobsenz, 1974; Levin and Levin, 1975). Older women report less interest in sexual activity than do younger women, and less than men of comparable ages; however, they also report that the interest in sexual activity is greater than the amount of sexual activity (Pfeiffer, Verwoerdt, and Wang, 1968; Pfeiffer, Verwoerdt, and Davis, 1972).

Why the decline in activity and satisfaction? Part of the reason is obviously physical. The biological organism ages, and changes in physiological response patterns emerge. Dr. Weg has discussed these changes in another chapter of this book. Health and feelings of vitality and vigor are important. The ill body is not as responsive as the healthy one, and those in ill health report less interest in sex and less sexual activity than those in good health. Insofar as aging is related to increasing likelihood of physical debilities, some changes in sexual activity are predictable and can be seen as "normal" (Rossman, 1975).

The link beteen sexual activity and health may be reciprocal. That is, sexual activity, being good exercise, has been linked to better health in warding off arthritic pains, heart attacks, and depression, and in preserving general bodily vitality (Scheingold and Wagner, 1974). An intriguing observation by a physician is that the physiological effects of the most commonly used drugs in institutions were similar in effects to sexual orgasm; he suggests reducing unacceptable and pathological behavior by giving genital massages rather than drugs (Kassel, 1974).

However, biological changes are not sufficient to account for all the altered patterns in later years. At all ages, people with medical disabilities continue to function sexually, and the range of individual variation is great. A number of factors besides physical aging are important and will be discussed below: the significance of the differences in the meanings of sexuality (1) between women and men, and (2) over historical periods, and (3) the incentives for sexual behavior.

Any activity will be largely satisfying insofar as it meets the expectations and needs of the participants. It is obvious that sexual activities and sexuality in general have varied meanings and that these may differ over time, situation, and generation. For example, it is traditionally said that American women emphasize the emotional aspects of sexual activities, the sense of closeness, sharing, and cuddling that accompanies intercourse, and that men are traditionally pictured as valuing more the physical aspects. Thus men may be unable to meet their partners' desires for a social-sexual relationship. Many men are uncomfortable with women's demands for psychological intimacy. Such emotionally constricted men may find almost any expectations "excessive," and this would affect their sexual relationships. Since older men are often less defensive about their masculinity and more open to their needs for nurturance than are younger men, this could make them better sexual partners. On the other hand, older men often have years of "bad habits" with long-time partners, and are unable to change their ways of relating that would make them more satisfying partners.

An obstacle to the ability of older women to meet the sexual needs of older men is the idea that manual and oral-genital pleasuring is "deviant." An older man with normal age changes in sexual responsivity often needs, and wants, prolonged genital caressing, and he may become more appreciative of total body sensuality (Kaplan, 1974). Even when he cannot achieve an erection sufficient for vaginal intercourse, mutual pleasure is very possible with massage and oral stimulation. However, few older women feel comfortable with these expressions of sexuality.

Some differences in goals or meanings of sex between young people and old people reflect the fact that different historical periods have defined and regulated human sexual responses in varied ways. Female orgasmic responses, for example, have been culturally shaped in different ways in different periods. Where there are cultural expectations that women will "naturally" be orgasmic with appropriate stimulation, men are instructed in proper techniques and women accept orgasms as their due pleasure. On the other hand, vast numbers of women may also appear nonorgasmic if the prevailing culture dictates that women do not have sexual feelings, that sexual release is extra- ordinary, and that female sexuality is only for the service of procreation and the convenient release of male needs. We are experiencing a marked shift now toward expecting (even demanding) female orgasmic response. This was not true for the women who are now old, as they were growing up. Women who are middle-aged seem to be caught in the middle of this change in expectations.

Historical periods and cultures also differ in age norms — what behaviors are regarded as appropriate and desirable for individuals of a particular age. For example, one of the clearest changes has been the increasing acceptance of (and pressure for) premarital sexual activity among college and even high school students. Currently, the longstanding norms against older woman-younger man couples and against romance among the elders are being challenged (Delilah, 1975).

Even with adequate biological capability, there must also be incentives for behaving sexually. An understanding of these incentives is crucial to understanding sexuality and aging. Only rarely is "species survival" or even motherhood the governing force for women today, if indeed it ever was.

One set of motives involves release of sexual tensions generated by contact and by stimulation of the genitals. This viewpoint is expressed by those who explain that they engage in sexual activity simply because "it's natural." In one sample of elderly nursing home residents, this was the most common reason given, but both men and women agreed that men were more likely to engage in sexual activities for this reason (Loeb and Wasow, 1975). Such sexual tensions may be related to androgenic hormone levels. As these decline among some older men they report decreased sexual tension. Clinicians report that elderly women, particularly those taking replacement hormone therapy, may be bothered by such needs (Kassel, 1974).

One reason that older women may be bothered by such physical sensations is that female sexuality has not, until fairly recently in our culture, been defined in terms of biological need. The generations of women who are now old grew up in times when sexual "needs" of women were defined in terms of reproduction and providing pleasure for others. With such a perspective, it is difficult to recognize and acknowledge sexual tensions that seem to be self-generated, that are not part of an acceptable relationship, and that appear to have no function other than personal release from tension, and, possibly, pleasure. In fact, the pleasure may often be questionable since it is mixed with guilt for women who do not see their sexual urges as legitimate, honorable, and joyous. If they are embarrassed by the feelings in their genitals and by their felt needs for arousal and orgasm, their resultant satisfaction is diminished.

Another incentive for sexual activity is contact comfort, the kind of touching, stroking, and fondling that has been well-documented as crucial for the well-being of rats and infants. This is undoubtedly important for the well-being of older adults, as well. As one 45- year-old woman said,

> Honestly, I find it very hard to imagine life 10, 15 years from now without a child in my life. I have a physical need for daily contact with someone I love. I'm truly realistic in knowing that as an old or older woman, I'm not going to get physical love from anyone but a child. No one wants to touch an old person, no one except the very young. One of the sad things about getting old is you lose a chance for phsyical contact with people because everyone has decided you are ugly (Dreifus, 1973, p. 251).

"The skin you love to touch" is, in our culture, soft and supple and young. Our idealistic concept links sex, love, and romance with health and beauty. Physical beauty and fitness are seen as the precursors to "love," and love to sex; this often rules out of competition or gratification the disabled, the homely, and the elderly—who are, by definition, assumed to be homely.

Furthermore, our culture generally taboos touching contact except as a prelude to sexual activity. Touching between women and men, especially, is assumed to be a nonverbal signal for sexual negotiation. These expectations make it difficult to gratify needs for touching and contact comfort outside a sexual encounter, and make it even more difficult for the older person to obtain such gratification.

A common theme in the research and adjustment literature is that older women do fine sexually as long as they have "regular and effective sexual stimulation" (Masters and Johnson, 1966). How does one obtain this magic antidote to the more prevalent sense of rejection and despair among older women? What are the options for sexual expression for older women?

One option, available and exercised from infancy through old age, is self-pleasuring. Babies soon discover the sensual delights of fabric against skin, of touching the genitals; they continue unless and until they learn such pleasures are "bad." Adolescents masturbate, adults do it, even married ones, and older people do it. At its best, this can be a very gratifying enterprise—taking time for yourself, time to explore your body and appreciate its uniqueness and the pleasurable sensations it provides. You are in charge of the pacing of stimulation, and you can vary the patterning to maximize pleasurable feelings. Orgasm can come quickly or after prolonged play. Your mind can wander and indulge in whatever fantasies turn you on— memories of past sensual times, of imagined partners, of color and harmony.

However, it is not easy for many women to enjoy masturbation—even if it is called "self-love." First, some women have difficulty loving themselves, particularly as the skin wrinkles, the breasts sag, and the waist thickens. Nothing in the mirror affirms the cultural ideals of physical feminine beauty. What, therefore, is "lovable"? In addition, women have been taught since childhood that sexuality was to be "saved," only to be shared with a partner of longstanding commitment, or at least within the confines of a love relationship. Women did not grow up learning they had feelings and sexual needs of their own, and that it was good to explore their own bodies for pleasurable possibilities. As a result, most women today feel guilty about masturbation. Some younger women are struggling with these feelings in consciousness-raising and therapy groups, trying to feel free enough to give themselves pleasure. Older women generally do not like to talk about it or admit they might engage in such activities. Few older women are able to really enjoy masturbation, or regard it as a genuine alternative for sexual expression. Most older women who have discussed it refer to it as a sort of last resort, something to do when the biological urges for release get overwhelming. The shame and loneliness that many women (and men) report after masturbating reflects their sense that sexuality is defined by sharing, and further, that sexual pleasure must be "given" by another in order to be legitimate. Masturbating can seem like giving yourself a Valentine, final testimony that you are so unworthy that no one else will bother with you.

Some older women, and younger single women, do express a preference for masturbation as an alternative to a poor partner. They often make the decision to stick to masturbating after they have tried sex with partners whose use of sex blocks the possibility of any good relationship. Such women may decide that self-pleasure is better than feeling used or abused in a relationship (Edwards and Hoover, 1974).

For most men and women, sexual expression is still considered best within a partnership. Older women particularly want sex in a legally sanctioned, loving relationship, as an expression of commitment and caring, with tenderness and sharing an integral part of the sexual aspects of the relationship. What are the probabilities that this will be available to older women? Not very great, if we are to believe the data available.

First, the chances increase with every decade of age that older women will not be in a legally recognized marriage. Death, divorce, and desertion all take their toll.

In addition, any sexual encounter involves risk, and the communication is often largely nonverbal. These aspects make sexual negotiations delicate. Negotiation over sexual encounters occurs in marriage and out. Within a marriage relationship, particularly one of long duration, the partners have the advantage of experience in accurately "reading" nonverbal communications. There is a sense of comfort and ease that characterizes many long-term marriages. At best, this sense of ease and comfort extends to the sexual relationship. No single sexual encounter is terribly important, because there will be others. In old age, the experiences are tinged with memories of past shared pleasures (and pains). Each partner may not see what an outsider would see, but an image blending the youthful past with the altered present. For single women, such negotiations are even more difficult.

For most in our culture, and certainly for most older women, sexuality is laden with emotional meanings. We stand stripped, often literally naked, open to the gaze of our partner. There is the looming question, will I pass inspection? The aging woman is not regarded as beautiful in our culture; the ability to arouse passion (and penises) is assumed to be the prerogative of firm, shapely young women. To the extent that older women themselves believe that they are not sexy—or assume that their partner will not see them as thus—any sexual encounter means risking outright rejection. Few of us want to experience rejection. This rejection can be entirely nonverbal and very subtle—the cast of the eyes, the avoidance of prolonged touch, the quick separation after the act is over. Worse, the individual who expects and anticipates such rejection may perceive it when it is not, in fact, intended or "really there." This may mean that older women anticipate and experience rejection in sexual encounters even when it is unintended by their partner. This can be a severe problem in a marriage relationship. As one geriatric screening team found in interviewing over-65 couples, "when an elderly woman devalues herself it can be next to impossible for her spouse, with his diminished reserves of life energy, to buoy her flagging self-image" (Genavay, 1975, p. 69).

We must not overlook the potential that an older man is dealing with. He, too, is aging. His body sags. His responses are slowed, and he may anticipate and fear sexual rejection as much as or more than the woman. He may be alert to subtle signs of imagined or real repulsion, pity, indulgence. One defense against rejection is to be the first to reject. The unfortunate cycle has been documented by marriage and sex counselors, where the man fears "failures" of impotence and thus avoids his partner in order to avoid failure, and she assumes he has lost interest in her, has found another partner, or finds her repulsive, and is hurt, vengeful, and depressed. Acting on these feelings, the man in turn feels rejected, hurt, vengeful. This may help account for the finding that both men and women attributed the decline or cessation of sexual activity in later years to the man (Pfeiffer, Verwoerdt, and Davis, 1972).

Thus, older single women may have a difficult time finding a partner and negotiating an acceptable relationship. For some women, "acceptability" means that the man will not press sexual activities in addition to companionship. As one woman said, "I've had enough of that, and that's the trouble with most men anyway." Such women are not bothered by the sexual deprivation of their single state. They may welcome the attentions that serve to reaffirm femininity—flirting, touching, holding doors, commenting on new clothes and hairdos—but they do not want to carry it further. Some such women may be very attractive to older men; and younger women may wonder why they are attractive and how they can resist marriage to one of the suitors. However, as one popular woman, 64 years old, pointed out, she enjoyed going dancing, but told no one her last name or her address because she feared becoming entangled with another man who might be as unreliable and destructive as her former husband.

Some older single women would like to have sexual relationships with men, but find it difficult or impossible to do so. The norms still dictate that women should be involved sexually with men their age or older; this leaves an increasingly small pool of potential partners for women as they age. The older woman does not have the status value as a visible partner that younger, attractive women have. It is unlikely that she will be approached, almost automatically, as a potential sexual partner by men. Even if she wishes to develop a sexual relationship, the negotiations may be awkward, and men may resist mightily if she takes the initiative. Men who are now middle-aged or older have been socialized to believe that they should take the initiative in sexual encounters, and that the responsibility for the outcome was largely their responsibility. While many have complained to clinicians and to their friends about this responsibility, it left the balance of power in their hands. As long as they were in charge of initiating and monitoring the sexual exchange, they did not need to feel coerced to "perform." After all, there is nothing less responsive to compulsion and command than a limp penis. Thus, even though it may be true that men in later life experience less anxiety, on an intrapsychic level, about their own needs for nurturance and their passive inclinations (Gutmann, 1964, 1975), they may still have difficulty shifting their conscious set of expectations to feel comfortable with female initiative and demands. As one 79-year-old widower explained, "I just can't respond when she [a neighbor widow] comes up and says, 'Let's go fuck— I'm sorry to ask, but I'm tired of waiting around for you to ask me.'" One can sympathize with the feelings of this honest man, but also recognize that he has no comprehension of how difficult it is for the women around him to deal with their sexual desires within the system.

Some single women value sexual relationships in their later years, and manage to have them, but the extent of such behavior is not clear. One 69-year-old grandmother, divorced for nearly twenty years, has emerged sexually in the past two decades. During her marriage, she had frequent intercourse with her husband but no orgasms. She felt she could not let her husband know that she enjoyed these experiences. She is now in excellent physical shape, and has found dancing a good way to meet men. She finds older men very romantic and believes they express jealousy and devotion in a style reminiscent of adolescence. She likes to "try out" potential suitors sexually, since she values potency now that she has become orgasmic. She declared that any future husband should be sexually potent, a good dancer, able to mow the grass, nonalcoholic, nonparanoid, and have his own money. To her moralistic friends who want romance but worry about their reputation, she replies, "The worms won't care."

For those fortunate enough to have a sexual partner in later life, there are problems too. One potentially disabling aspect of even good marriage relationships is that they become stagnant and are no longer open to growth and change in the partners. Once issues have become "settled," one of the partners may be reluctant to challenge the status quo by bringing up new needs. There is ample evidence that women, for example, find it difficult to assert their sexual needs as they emerge in the second half of life. Most couples, particularly those who are now older, "settled" the issues of sexuality by assigning responsibility for interest and initiation to the husband. As the wife emerges into full sexual awareness and responsiveness in early middle age, she may feel very uncomfortable declaring her needs, her interests, or her desire to share new patterns. She may assume (correctly or not) that her husband would be threatened and keep silent, or indicate her displeasure with the sexual relationship in other areas that are not directly related to sexuality. Whatever patterns emerge during the middle years are likely to persist in the later years of marriage.

Older women are often in marriages that are not warm, comfortable, and gratifying. The atmosphere in these relationships is often one of resignation—given the dismal alternatives, the marriage relationship is at least no worse. In such relationships, sexual contact and fulfillment may be nil, or sexual contact may exist to be endured. Husbands may use sex, in later years as in earlier, as an expression of hostility or power, and sexual encounters then become another arena for playing out more basic problems in the relationship. Women may have used sex for reassurance or as a weapon for gaining power in the relationship. However, these uses are increasingly less viable for women as they age, since their husband may well stop desiring them enough to bargain for their sexual attentions. Thus, women who have used sex as a power weapon may find themselves isolated from men.

Some older married women find sexual gratifications in relationships outside marriage. Some discover their own sensuality and responsiveness only in their late middle years. One 50-year-old woman, long married to a man who shared his sexuality with a mistress, entered into her first affair (with a 66-year-old colleague) during a professional convention. She wrote her new lover lyrical poems and letters about the joys of "being reborn." Many women fantasize such affairs, but lack the opportunity, fear the consequences, or do not want to deal with the guilt that would accompany the pleasures.

The importance of loving attention is stressed in this little ditty by Irene Burnside (1968, p. 45):

> *The pill, the pill—now here's the truth:*
> *We don't need it to keep our youth.*
> *All we need is love and men;*
> *That's better than a dose of estrogen.*[1]

Agreeing with this conclusion, a hopeful tone characterizes Olga Knopf's advice for successful aging:

> A woman need not be a [famous mistress] to retain her attractiveness to men as the years go by. A good head on a woman's shoulders and a good education, as well as the ability to support herself or at least to contribute to the family treasury, give her a different status in the eyes of men, which substantially extends the years of her attractiveness to them. With education and work experience, women have been developing self-esteem and learning to meet men on their own ground. . . . (1975, p. 110)

The above messages share a common theme: women must remain attractive to men as they grow older if they are to remain good human beings. Sexuality is heterosexual, and improvement in female health, vitality, and attractiveness are important partly because they increase the likelihood that we will remain acceptable companions for older men. This is a reality for most women, to be

[1]From Revy Wikler and Peg S. Grey, *Sex and the Senior Citizen* (New York: Frederick Fell Publishers, Inc.). Copyright 1968 by Revy Wikler and Peg S. Grey. Reprinted by permission.

sure, and is not likely to change. Most women look to relationships with men to affirm (or deny) their feminine sexuality.

However, we must recognize that some women have long shared love, companionship, and sexuality with other women. They continue to do so in later years, although we know almost nothing about their pleasures and problems with aging. In addition, some women find they can share these aspects of living with both men and women. This is a rare pattern among women who are now elderly. It is a more common pattern among young, well-educated women. It remains to be seen whether women who genuinely like themselves and other women will find bisexuality a reasonable, viable alternative, particularly during the later years of life.

Women who are now middle-aged and young may have different experiences with their sexuality as they grow older. For example, Jessie Bernard writes enthusiastically about the New Woman:

> Something new has been added in recent years. A genuinely new biological subsex has been added to the human stock of sexes. A new kind of woman. She is the result of cultural forces, technological as well as normative, and of advances in medicine, nutrition, and health care, especially obstetrical. She was not designed and shaped for a specific function, as some other manufactured subsexes were. She was, in fact, an unanticipated consequence of modern science. . . .
>
> The New Women today are new . . . not in the sense that they are young, for they are not; they may be in their fifties and even their sixties. They are new in the sense that women like them have never existed on this planet until now. Their very existence is a brand new human and therefore social phenomenon—as a whole generation, that is; there have always been such individuals. . . . They are attractive, though not in the youthful way. They are not trying to look young. . . . Today there are attractive clothes designed for all ages. And the new women have the bodies to wear them. . . . The ability to be attractive is almost as much a cultural as a biological phenomenon. . . . The same forces are at work to improve the beauty of the new women as well as the young. In addition, social changes are in process which make it legitimate and proper for them to be attractive. Even to have sex appeal. When women in the middle years were treated as neuter it was difficult for them to act as women, like sexual beings. They may now be viewed as sexual as well as human beings. (1972, p. 25)

It is probable that as the young women of today age, they will remain concerned about their own sexual fulfillment. The evidence suggests that they, more than their mothers or grandmothers, value physical aspects of sexuality, are more assertive in sexual relationships, experiment with a variety of pleasuring techniques, see sexuality in terms of exploring their own sexual potential and for their own personal fulfillment, and are not so likely to confine sexual relationships within a legal marriage relationship, either before or after marriage (Bell and Lobsenz, 1974; Hunt, 1974; Levin and Levin, 1975; Levin, 1975). It is possible, though not necessarily so, that these patterns will make sexuality a less problematic aspect of living as they grow older.

The realities of everyday living are harsh for many older women, and a sense of sexual deprivation is but one of many pains. However, there are older women whose own sense of reality is joyful, who do not particularly wish to turn back the clock, and who feel good about their past and their current abilities to deal evenly with life. Some enjoy their sensual pleasures almost secretly, so as not to jar our youthful stereotypes of miserable old age. The agonies and ecstacies of love, romance, and sex persist, are rediscovered, or warm the reminiscence of times past. Youth is not all; as the elderly gentleman in one cartoon says to his equally toothless partner: "Do you know what I like about you, Rachael? You're old, like me."

REFERENCES

Bernard, Jessie, *The Sex Game: Communication Between the Sexes.* New York: Atheneum, 1972.

Bell, Robert, and Norman Lobsenz, "Married Sex: How Uninhibited Can a Woman Dare to Be?", *Redbook,* September 1974.

Burnside, Irene, "Sexuality and the Older Adult: Implications for Nursing," in *Sexuality and Aging,* ed. Irene Burnside, pp. 26-34. Los Angeles: Andrus Gerontology Center, 1975.

Calderone, Mary S., "The Status of Women, 1993-1998: Sexual/Emotional Aspects," in *No Longer Young: The Older Woman in America.* University of Michigan, Institute of Gerontology, Occasional Papers in Gerontology, No. 11, 1975, pp. 111-115.

Delilah, *Older Woman, Younger Man: The New Look in Love.* New York: Pinnacle Books, 1975.

Dreifus, Claudia, *Women's Fate.* New York: Bantam Books, 1973.

Edwards, Marie, and Eleanor Hoover, *The Challenge of Being Single.* New York: New American Library, Signet Books, 1974.

Gebhard, Paul, "Postmarital Coitus Among Widows and Divorcees," in *Divorce and After,* ed. Paul Bohanan. Garden City, N.Y.: Doubleday Anchor, 1971.

Genevay, Bonnie, "Age is Killing Us Softly . . . When We Deny the Part of Us Which is Sexual," in *Sexuality and Aging,* ed. Irene Burnside, pp. 67–75. Los Angeles: Andrus Gerontology Center, 1975.

Gutmann, David, "An Exploration of Ego Configurations in Middle and Later Life," in *Personality in Middle and Later Life,* ed. B. Neugarten. New York: Atherton, 1964.

_____"Parenthood: Key to the Comparative Psychology of the Life Cycle?" in *Life-Span Developmental Psychology,* eds. L. Ginsberg and N. Datan. New York: Academic Press, 1975.

Hunt, Morton, *Sexual Behavior in the 1970s.* Chicago: The Playboy Press, 1974.

Kaplan, Helen, *The New Sex Therapy.* New York: Brunner/Mazel, 1974. (a)

_____, "The Classification of the Female Sexual Dysfunctions," *Journal of Sex and Marital Therapy,* 1, No. 2, (Winter 1974), pp. 124–138. (b)

Kassel, Victor, comments included in notes from workshop in Sexuality and Alternative Life Styles, at 26th Conference on Aging, published in *No Longer Young: The Older Woman in America,* by the Institute of Gerontology of the University of Michigan and Wayne State University, 1974, pp. 5–9.

Kinsey, A. C., W. B. Pomeroy, C. E. Martin, and P. H. Gebhard, *Sexual Behavior in the Human Female.* Philadelphia: W. B. Saunders, 1953.

Knopf, Olga, *Successful Aging: The Facts and Fallacies of Growing Old.* New York: Viking Press, 1975.

Levin, Robert, and Amy Levin, "Sexual Pleasure: The Surprising Preferences of 100,000 Women," *Redbook,* September 1975.

Levin, Robert J., "The End of the Double Standard?", *Redbook,* October 1975.

Loeb, Martin, and Mona Wasow, "Sexuality in Nursing Homes," in *Sexuality and Aging,* ed. Irene Burnside, pp. 35–41. Los Angeles: Andrus Gerontology Center, 1975.

Masters, W. H., and V. Johnson, *Human Sexual Response.* Boston: Little, Brown, 1966.

_____, *Human Sexual Inadequacy.* Boston: Little, Brown, 1970.

Pfeiffer, E., "Sexual Behavior in Old Age," in *Behavior and Adaptation in Late Life,* eds. E. Busse and E. Pfeiffer. Boston: Little, Brown & Co., 1969.

Pfeiffer, Eric, and Glenn Davis, "Determinants of Sexual Behavior in Middle and Old Age," *Journal of American Geriatrics,* 20, No. 4 (April 1972), 151–158.

Pfeiffer, E., A. Verwoerdt, and H. Wang, "Sexual Behavior in Aged Men and Women," *Archives of General Psychiatry,* 19, No. 12 (1968), 753–58.

Pfeiffer, E., A. Verwoerdt, and G. Davis, "Sexual Behavior in Middle Life," *American Journal of Psychiatry,* 128, No. 10 (April 1972), pp. 1262–67.

Rossman, Isadore, "Sexuality and the Aging Process: An Internist's Perspective," in *Sexuality and Aging,* d. Irene Burnside, pp. 18–25. Los Angeles: Andrus Gerontology Center, 1975.

Scheingold, Lee, and Nathaniel Wagner, *Sound Sex and the Aging Heart.* New York: Behavioral Publications, Inc., 1974.

Verwoerdt, A., E. Pfeiffer, and H. Wang, "Sexual Behavior in Senescence," in *Normal Aging,* d. E. Palmer. Durham, N.C.: Duke University Press, 1969, pp. 282–98.

Chapter 5

Does Youthfulness
Equal Attractiveness?

Carol A. Nowak

To be "old" in this society is certainly not good. But to be an "old bag" is decidedly worse. Getting old happens to everyone. Becoming shapeless, wrinkled, and unattractive happens to women. Just ask anybody. While middle-aged men with "touches of gray" look "distinguished," women who haven't "colored away the gray" look drab. While middle-aged men with "lines" and "furrows" have "character," middle-aged women with "wrinkles" and "crow's feet" look ugly. While middle-aged men are generally taken for a handsome lot, middle-aged women are typically judged as "over the hill." And middle-aged women themselves are most guilty of perpetuating these expectations. They are their own worse critics.

At first I expected that *old* women would be hardest hit by the "old bag" syndrome. It seemed to me that they were the ones who were guilty of violating two of society's most sacred commandments—"Thou shalt be young" and "Thou shalt be beautiful." They were the ones hit by the double whammy of lost youth and waning physical attractiveness, and might therefore be expected to be depressed, dissatisfied, and self- derogatory. Many studies find the same stereotypes of old age. (These have been reviewed elsewhere by Troll and Nowak, 1976) Old people are sup

Carol A. Nowak, Ph.D., is a psychologist at Pennsylvania State University. She is currently continuing research on sex differences in the importance of appearance.

posed to be listless, isolated, boring, dependent, unexciting, unintelligent, and dull. But so, suggests the interpersonal attraction literature, are physically unattractive people. (See, for example, the studies of Kirkpatrick and Cotton, 1951; Dion, Berscheid, and Walster, 1972, and Nowak, 1975). They, too, are supposed to be unpopular, inactive, unappealing, joyless, clinging, old-looking, and subdued. To be old, and to look old, then, are two very uncomplimentary things—especially for women. For while men and women must both grow old and appear physically as if they have aged, it is the latter that is especially disturbing for women. From childhood on, a woman is impressed with the importance of a youthful, attractive appearance. A woman must be attractive to "catch" her man, and attractive to keep him. She must be attractive to be clever, and attractive to be arousing. Her husband, and therefore her marriage, will be happier if she doesn't "let herself go," and her social credibility is greater the better she looks. Men, on the other hand, are spared such attributions. But even if they were not, they would have little to worry about. Some of my recent research indicates that men and women both agree that a man's attractiveness is enhanced by age. When an aging woman successfully defends herself against the negative stereotypes of old age, then, she has won only half of the battle; the man who does so is a declared victor. A woman must still reconcile herself to her looks.

Much to my surprise, I found no support for my expectations that old women lament either their age or their looks. In fact, I found just the opposite. A great deal of evidence has been accumulated to suggest that old people might hold the stereotypes about old age when they describe "other old people, in general," but certainly not when speaking about themselves. Furthermore, most old people don't even consider themselves old, but rather young or middle-aged. (See, for example, the studies of Tuckman and Lorge, 1954; Zola, 1962; Kastenbaum and Durkee, 1964; and Streib, 1968). And finally, my own explorations suggest that looking old and unattractive is among the least of the concerns that older women have. I at first found it difficult to believe that older women—the target group of two potent societal norms to maintain youth and perpetuate beauty—were apparently as unaffected by having grown old as they seemed. While most investigators attribute this finding to "denial" of growing old, I came to believe that it might instead reflect a true lack of concern for these stereotypic worries. Maybe a middle-aged woman's *anticipation* of lost youth and beauty is far more distressing than the actual extent of such "damages" in old age. It could be that the perceived transition into old age by a woman in midlife prompts confusion and disillusionment not only in how she views her own age and attractiveness, but in how she judges these same attributes in others. It seems from my own research that the triggering event of this transitional period of concern for the midlife woman is the unwelcome debut of the first noticeable wrinkle!

Some preliminary research I conducted suggests that at no other time in a woman's life does there seem to be as high a concern with facial attractiveness as during middle age. Women who are younger or older describe themselves in a variety of ways and can assess their physical attributes independently from their activities, interests, and feelings. Middle-aged women, particularly those beteen 45 and 55, are less able to separate appearance from feelings. It is as if their concerns about age- related changes in their looks interfere with how objectively they can judge themselves on other qualities and characteristics. The midlife woman who has begun to notice a new wrinkle or sag begins to worry about things like "not being up on what's happening today," "being rather boring and unexciting lately," "having doubts about her husband's interest in her," and "not getting out and involved as much as she probably should." She is too often ready to write off her youth along with her looks. And she is also apt to blame herself for having let all this happen to her. In short, while women under 45 are more concerned with their attractiveness but seldom see this affecting their youthfulness, and while women over 65 worry in just the opposite direction, middle-aged women clearly worry about both. When they begin to *see* that they have begun to age, they confuse this perception with perceptions about their attractiveness.

The next step in my research plan was to see whether middle-aged women "suffer in silence," or if they tend instead to project their own changes onto others. I reasoned that a possible test of whether people vary by age in the extent to which they separate attractiveness from youthfulness would be to vary both of these dimensions independently in a group of target individuals whom I would then ask my subjects to rate for "looks" and for "youthfulness." If middle-aged women seriously believe that they can defer the negative consequences of aging by continuing to look attractive, then they should judge attractive women as more youthful than unattractive women, no matter what age they are said to be. They should also show greater distortion of this kind than either younger or older subjects. Just to be sure that midlife women are the misperceivers, I also included men in this study, both as subjects and as targets to be evaluated.

The first problem I encountered was how to define such nebulous aspects of appearance as "attractiveness" and "youthfulness." While I had to acknowledge that attractiveness can be more than physical, I finally decided to define it as the visual-aesthetic component of appearance. That is, attractiveness was based upon how "good" or how "bad" people look, without making presumptions about mannerisms, behaviors, or personality attributes. I used three-quarter view color slides, face only, of men and women who were "made up" by photographers, and prejudged by raters, to look "attractive," "plain," or "unattractive." Youthfulness, on the other hand, was defined as the interpretation of others' looks in terms of age-related characteristics, and might or might not be independent of how attractive they were perceived to be. Judgments about the youthfulness of "attractive," "plain," and "unattractive" people of various ages were made on the basis of how old they looked, what their interests were presumed to be, and how active they probably were.

Having decided on these dimensions, I next divided 240 men and women equally by age and by sex into either a "control" or one of three experimental conditions. Ten young-, middle-, and late-adult men and women were in each group. The average age of the young adults was about 25; middle adults, 48; and late adults, 69. People in all conditions were shown fifty-four face-view slides of young-, middle-, and late-adult men and women who had previously been judged, as described earlier, to be "attractive," "plain," or "unattractive." The men and women whose attitudes I was studying were then asked to rate each of the pictures on youthfulness and attractiveness. Depending on the experimental group to which they had been assigned, I told them either the model's actual age, an age ten years older, ten years younger than the actual age, or gave no age at all.

As I'd expected, middle-aged women, significantly more than anybody else—all men or younger or older women—judged the most "attractive" models, regardless of their age, to be most youthful. The highest ratings for attractiveness were given by the middle-aged women to the women in the picture who had been presented as being ten years older than they actually were. (These women thus looked young for their supposed age.) As far as middle-aged women are concerned, the younger one looks, the better one looks, and the more youthful, of course, one is presumed to be. It is not surprising, then, that middle-aged women agreed that young adult women were the most attractive women of all.

It was also very interesting that when middle-aged women were rating either "attractive" or "unattractive" middle-aged women in the pictures, the attractiveness of the "attractive" was minimized and the unattractiveness of the "unattractive" was exaggerated. For no other group did this kind of pattern emerge. It seems that a middle-aged woman can never look truly attractive to another middle-aged woman, but she certainly can look ugly. And the same goes for her youthfulness. Middle-aged women perceived pictures of middle-aged women as much less youthful than anybody else. Women of other ages (and men of all ages) were much more objective. There seems little question that the middle-aged woman's turmoil about her own youthfulness and attractiveness spills over into how she views people whom she perceives as similar in plight to herself.

While the poor middle-aged woman is in such a state of self-derogation and confusion, then, what is happening to her middle-aged male counterpart? Something quite different. Far from emerging the underdog in the battle for youth and beauty, just about everybody agrees that the middle-aged male is at the epitome of his looks and vigor. There is very little about him, in fact, judged to be old or ugly. Surely this state of affairs, coupled with the midlife male's generally high level of self-esteem, adds yet another harassment to the transitional flux of the midlife woman. If beauty is indeed in the eye of the beholder, what's a middle-aged woman to do? It seems that she will have to accept her own aging before she can once more perceive herself as attractive. The sooner the midlife transition is passed, then, the better.

REFERENCES

Dion, D., E. Berscheid, and E. Walster, *"What Is Beautiful Is Good,"* *Journal of Personality and Social Psychology*, 24, No. 3 (1972), 285-90.

Kastenbaum, R., and N. Durkee, "Young People View Old Age," in *New Thoughts on Old Age*, ed. R. Kastenbaum, pp. 237-49. New York: Springer, 1964.

Kirkpatrick, C., and J. Cotton, "Physical Attractiveness, Age, and Marital Adjustment," *American Sociological Review*, 16 (1951), 81-86.

Nowak, C., "The Appearance Signal in Adult Development," unpublished doctoral dissertation, Wayne State University, 1975.

Streib, G., "Are the Aged a Minority Group?", in *Middle Age and Aging*, ed. B. Neugarten, pp. 35-46. Chicago: University of Chicago Press, 1968.

Troll, L., and C. Nowak, "How Old Are You? The Question of Age Bias in the Counseling of Adults," *The Counseling Psychologist*, 16 (1976), 41-44.

Tuckman, J., and I. Lorge, "Classification of the Self as Young, Middle-Aged, or Old," *Geriatrics* (1954), 534-36.

Zola, I., "Feelings About Age in Older People," *Journal of Gerontology* (1962), pp. 65-68.

Chapter 6

Confessions
of a 45-Year-Old Feminist

Joan Israel

I always believed in the saying "mind over matter"—that is, until the last few months. I was under the impression that I would never mind growing older because I didn't look my age. Ever since I can remember, people have thought I was years younger. It was easy to be casual about being middle-aged. Besides, I was a feminist, and didn't that mean that concern about appearance was trivial? Ideologically, I was not supposed to be buying the Great American Sexist Dream about youth, slimness, and big bosoms. Not only was I not buying it for myself, but I was doing everything I could to see that no one else bought it. I became a feminist therapist, helping other women explore new facets of themselves so that they would not be dependent on youth and beauty for feeling good about themselves or secure with the men in their lives. I organized conferences on aging women to alert teachers and researchers in gerontology to the double standard of aging. So, if I was so clearly dedicated to feminism and the more significant aspects of women's character—besides looking young and therefore beautiful while I did so—if I was going around raising everyone's consciousness, why should I worry about my own? I would be one of

Joan Israel, ACSW, is a psychotherapist in Detroit, Michigan and a member of the National Board of the National Organization for Women. She is interested in a feminist approach to therapy and mental health and has led workshops and seminars in this area.

those model women who would age gracefully. I'd age with confidence, with security, with adventure.

Then one day, a few weeks after my 45th birthday, I looked in
the mirror and said to myself, "Joan, you look old!" The skin under
my chin and neck suddenly sagged and wrinkled. I had snickered at
Bea Arthur in "Maude" because of the high-necked outfits she wore
designed to cover her crepe neck, but I would snicker no more! I
tried pulling the skin to one side and agreed that this made me look
better (younger).

There I was, face to face with me. I did not like what I saw,
but I was finding it hard to admit this. I had never felt like this
before. I had always been happy with me: with my body, my face,
my skin.

After I got over the shock of my neck, I examined my hands.
Gee, they looked wrinkled! All of a sudden, there was a lot of gray in
my hair. My skin was dryer and flabbier. My breasts drooped.

But why was I so upset? Was this simply egotism? Would getting older mean I was less attractive as a person? Less attractive to
whom? To men in general? This had never been my bag, even when
I was younger. Less attractive to my husband? He gave no indication of being turned off. Maybe it was the promise of things to
come: aging, illness, death. I still do not know for sure. All I know is
I was overwhelmed with concern about getting old.

Now I found myself very curious to see whether other women
felt the way I did. My occasional professional reading in gerontology had never made this seem real to me. I had read Neugarten's
reports about age attitudes (Neugarten, 1968) but this seemed to
apply to some generalized women out there who would not be like
me in any essential way. So I sat down and made a list of questions.
I wanted to know how the women I knew—my feminist friends and
my middle-aged clients—felt about these matters. And I went
around asking as many of them as I could reach. I asked young
feminists and middle-aged feminists. I asked middle-aged
nonfeminists. Most of the women were in their 30s and 40s. I asked
them all the questions that were bothering me. About the things
they look forward to in the future. About how they feel about different parts of their body—their face, their skin, their arms, their
their hands, their sex organs, their breasts. I asked them how they
thought aging would affect their relationship with people closest to

them — their husband, their children, their parents. I asked them about their health, about their style of dress, their use of cosmetics. I even asked them where they expect to be living and what they expect to be doing when they are 50, 60, 70, 80. I had to know if they were experiencing the same things I was.

And I got many answers that interested me. For instance, one 27-year-old woman thought she would be old at 40. Many of the women in their 30s said that 30 was old — that was when they had gone "over the hill." On the other hand, there were women in their late 40s who said they were going to be old at 50. Just like me. I feel I am going to be old at 50, even though I realize 50 is only around the corner. I can remember when I thought 30 was "old" or "middle aged" — the same thing. Now 30 seems like a marvelous age to be. Yet, looking back, 30 was a time when I felt pressured to "get with it" before it was too late. It was a time when life decisions had to be made. I had to get going on my career. I had to deal with my marriage and my two children. So I and the other women I knew were doing just what has been reported in the literature.

In general, the younger women, those under 40, were more worried about losing attractiveness, and the older women, those over 40, were more concerned about health. Again, Neugarten's findings were repeated. This caught my attention. Since I was more concerned with the loss of appearance than with physical ills, did that mean that I am "youthful" for my age?

Why did the shock of aging come to me this year? Like the younger women I queried, I had not yet lost my skin tone or my hair color, nor in fact, any of the standards of attractiveness. Maybe I "woke up" later than most women. Maybe most women reach this point earlier in their 40s and by my age have already figured out how to cope with this. Perhaps they have started "corrective" measures — more cosmetics, for example. For me, the process had been postponed and I had deluded myself that it wouldn't happen to me!

Did my anxiety arise from confronting mortality? Was I afraid that dying was closer than I expected — that I wouldn't have enough time to do what I wanted to do? Like many women my age, I had had to face my parents' ill health, my father's death.

Was I worried about being alone in old age? My husband had had a heart attack two years earlier and I had thought he might not live. Like other women I had been socialized to avoid being alone. I saw myself as complete only when I was part of a twosome. Was it fear of possibly being alone that had led me to throw myself into a great flurry of activity, to try to achieve all the many things I had talked about but hadn't yet tackled?

I also discovered that aging was not all negative. I and the women I talked with were pleased with our experience and maturity, our professional success or status in the community. We were pleased that our children were getting to be on their own. Like the women studied by Neugarten, (1968) Lowenthal, Thurnher, and Chiriboga (1975), and others, we were far from depressed by "the empty nest" prospect. We looked forward to using our energy in new directions. Most of us, whether employed out of the home or not, generally looked forward to the future with pleasant anticipation.

Since the main purpose of the questions had been to see how common my own feelings about looking old were, I was interested to see that most of the women I asked showed generalized concern about wrinkled skin and drooping breasts and buttocks. The dream merchants, advertisers, cosmetics and foundation manufacturers know what they are doing. On the other hand, all of the women felt their sexual organs had improved with age and expected this would continue. Their main fear, like mine, was not that their sexual urge or capacity for enjoying sex would decrease but that their outward appearance would get in the way of finding a partner. They seemed to be saying, "It doesn't matter who I am, after all, just what I look like."

What does all of this have to do with me? How have the answers of other women affected me? I feel that aging has hit me and I have had to accept it. I also feel that I am lucky because I do not rely entirely upon appearance for feeling good.

It was good to share these feelings and concerns about myself. It makes me feel better and I can accept myself and my future better. "Rap groups" on aging can help.

After all, being a feminist and actively involved in changing other people's and society's attitudes toward aging has had a positive effect upon me.

In fact, now that I have looked inward, the next step for me is to look outward. I'm ready to expand my horizons. I want to try things I have always wanted to do.

REFERENCES

Lowenthal, M., M. Thurnher, and D. Chiriboga, *Four Stages of Life*. San Francisco: Jossey-Bass, 1975.

Neugarten, B., *Middle Age and Aging*. Chicago: University of Chicago Press, 1968.

PART III

The Soul

There are perhaps two kinds of intimacy, that of the body and that of the "soul." Both Ruth Weg and Margaret Hellie Huyck indicated that intimacy of the body is closely fused with intimacy of friendship, though their focus was upon the body. In the following section, the authors are generally concerned with what, for want of a better word, we might call the "soul." A woman's best friend may be her husband, but she may have other best friends, and none of her friends may be her husband. In fact, as Harold Feldman points out in his Narcissus type, and Florine Livson suggests more indirectly, her best friend may be herself. In this section we are dealing with love and fulfillment and satisfaction, largely of a nonphysical kind. What are some ways older women can find heightened meaning and pleasure in life?

Not much attention has been given to the importance of friendship patterns as women move through their middle and later years. The spontaneity of choosing girlfriends in childhood, the resultant camaraderie and sharing, is often replaced by a competition for male attention in adolescence. The friends of young mothers are often chosen from among the parents of their children's playmates. A night out with the girls has up to now not been institutionalized in the same way as "a night out with the boys." For those women who do not work outside the home and who rely upon their family for self-esteem, friends can be an important source of sup-

port and comfort. This is especially so when husbands are busy with careers and children grow up and strike off on their own.

When women choose to remain single, friends provide an available and acceptable network of social contacts. Women who move through social groups alone are oftentimes viewed with suspicion and as a threat.

For widows, "losing the man you were closest with makes you go back to earlier times, to the closeness you once had with your women friends."*

Incidentally, haven't we all been assuming the friends of women would be of the same sex?

*Joyce Maynard, New York Times, May 24, 1970.

Chapter 7

Penelope, Molly, Narcissus, and Susan

Harold Feldman

Before long, it will not be unusual for people to live for ninety years. It may be that our first third of life will involve preparation for adulthood, with commitment to family and school, and our second third will concern occupation and family. During the last third though we may be "free at last."

Members of the present generation of older people, because of the economic resources provided through pensions and retirement plans, have more freedom to live independently than did older people of the past, who often had to join the household of one of their children. Today's old people are also better educated and more adventurous. They have participated in the changes that have transformed our society, from the first telegraphic message to live TV from Mars. They have seen many medical advances that have directly affected their present state of health. Let us consider some ways in which these extra, healthier years can bring more meaning to life.

The four typologies I will describe represent four ways of living that are, of course, not mutually exclusive. Different patterns may be used at the same time or followed sequentially as circumstances

Harold Feldman, Ph.D., is in the Department of Human Development and Family Studies, Cornell University. In collaboration with Margaret Feldman, Ph.D., Professor of Psychology, Ithaca, College, he has been investigating marital satisfaction over the life span for many years and has numerous publications in this area. He is past president of the Groves Conference on the Family.

change. The labels are based on well-known real or mythological characters: Penelope, Molly, Narcissus, and Susan. Incidentally, these typologies need not be for women alone. Along with the new rise in feminist consciousness, both men and women can consider styles of living previously restricted to one or the other.

PENELOPE

The original Penelope was the wife of Ulysses. She was so truly in love with her husband that for many years she waited for the slim chance of his returning, refusing all others. The Penelopes of our time get their life meaning from their personal relationships with their husbands. In my 1973 study of the marriages of 852 couples, I found that the level of marital satisfaction of older persons, where the wife was at least 65 years old, corresponded to that of couples during their first two years of marriage.

The quality of the marriage is different during these periods. The new marriage is more exciting, with more emphasis on love, on talking about interpersonal relations, on sex, and interestingly, on relations with their parents. When young couples are in conflict situations, they focus on each other. They kiss or slap each other instead of kicking the furniture or slamming the door.

Those couples who have been married for many years are more companionate. They spend more of their time talking about adult topics such as the news and cultural events. When they come into conflict, they are more willing to forgive and forget than to keep harping on the topic.

Deutscher (1964) reported that only 10 percent of the postparental couples he interviewed said that the postparental period was in any way negative. Some of the advantages they mentioned were relief from financial responsibilities, ability to be geographically mobile, and greater freedom. As one woman said, "We no longer need to lead the self-consciously restricted existence of models for our children and can let our hair down. We can even serve food directly out of the pan."

These findings of happiness in the later years of marriage should be good news for the younger generation. If couples live long enough and can stick with their marriage, they may be able to realize the American dream of living happily ever after. Even though marriage might not remain so exciting, it can be good and provide companionship. For some couples, the road to this good end may be more difficult than for others. For some, their children's leaving may cause a difficult gap and they may need to form a new relationship with one another.

But what about those who are unmarried, either because they never married, were divorced, or became widowed? With the sex ratio being as it is among the elderly, they can have a serious problem. I'm not going to dwell on plural marriages or communal arrangements as ways for women to share a dwindling supply of men, although I do think they are reasonable alternatives to be explored. I would like to suggest that more women may find enjoyment with each other as companions. Perhaps more attention could be placed earlier in their lives on ways that women can share more with each other through significant relationships. If the most important characteristic of Penelopes is companionate relationships, it should be possible to turn to friends when husbands are not available.

MOLLY

The next type I have called Molly after Molly Goldberg, the "Jewish mamma." It is, of course, possible to be a Jewish mamma without being Jewish. The Mollys of this world find all their meaning in life through children. These women find it easy to turn to grandchildren and foster grandchildren and, in fact, any children for their source of happiness. One grandmother related this little vignette. She was saying goodby to her 3- year-old grandchild after having played with her. The little girl put her hand on her grandmother's arm, looked up at her, and said, "You know, Grandma, I think we are going to be good friends." This illustrates, in part, the tremendous potential that children have in affirming the lives of older persons. Perhaps we need to socialize children to be more positively expressive to their parents, rather than passive recipients of adult attention. Clavan and Vatter (1973) have suggested a cross-generational affiliative family, in which an older woman joins the family of a young woman who has small children but no husband. They can make a very satisfying family unit.

Children are so important to some older women, they are willing to conform to the demands made on them by their children even after the children have grown. We know a lot about how children are influenced by their parents while the children are young, but less about how children influence their parents (Osofsky and O'Connell, 1972; Feldman, 1971). Some of this influence is for the good. For example, my children have helped in my political education. But do children have the the right to make demands for conformity on their parents after they have grown? I know a rather young widow, under 60, who was interested in having an affair with a man without benefit of marriage but decided against it because her children did not approve. Older persons need to escape from the tyranny of their children.

Of course, not all older people are Mollys. Although relationships with children may be very satisfying, many parents are glad not to have children at home any more, to be free of some of the hassles of childrearing. They are delighted not to have to worry whether their children are on drugs, are pregnant, are doing well in school, have enough friends, will get a job, or will not be too rejecting of them, the parents. In fact, there is some evidence that one of the reasons older marriages do so well is that children have left home. The parents can use their money, even though it may be less, for their own pleasure. Even more important, their time and emotional energy can now be dedicated to one another. As one woman put it,

> My husband and I had drifted apart when the children were there. They seemed to need me more than he did. After all, my husband was an adult and they were little children. Recently we have started talking again. I just wasn't aware that he needed me. I thought his job was more important to him, and he thought I just didn't have time for him because I was involved with children. I'm glad I found out in time. These are the best years.

This period, when children are no longer at home, has been described as the "empty nest" period. I'm not an ornithologist, but it's my understanding that when the nest is empty and the young birds have left, so have their parents. The birds have flown off to new adventures.

NARCISSUS

Another alternative for the new generation is exemplified by Narcissus. If you remember, he loved himself so much that in leaning over the pool to look at himself he fell in and drowned. People in our society are not supposed to admire themselves. They are not supposed to be conceited. Indeed, what, many ask, do older persons have to be conceited about? How can they find meaning through looking at themselves and their life? Rollo May described self-love as follows:

> One of the good things about our progress in the past few years is that we've learned the value of self-love. This is not selfishness at all but really self-esteem. You ought to value yourself as much as you value others. That means love your neighbor as you love yourself, not love your neighbor as you hate yourself. Self-love is a necessary require-ment in order to love other people. (1973, pp. 55–56)

Perhaps the words at the wedding ceremony ought to be, "I love me truly so now I can love you too." How can older women get to love themselves in this positive way? One method is to look back on their life and say, "Well, it may not have been perfect, but it was good." The new generation of older women can start this process by reminding themselves that they have lived through greater technological change than any other generation ever has, and maybe ever will. They have lived through the time of the horse-drawn carriage, of no running water, no central heating, no elec-tricity, no jet planes, and no atomic bombs. Some of the women who read this book have fought for women's rights in their own way: in their own homes, or on the street, or by getting jobs that were not sex-typed. They changed fashion by cutting their hair in the '20s. They can surely be proud of participating in the revolution of change. Today's older women can compare themselves with their own parents and say that they have come a long way in their lifetime, educationally and occupationally. They will live longer and will participate more in the world around them.

Narcissus types frequently like to live alone. They may talk to themselves because they like talking to somebody interesting. The more they know about themselves, the better. They like doing what they want to do. They come to senior centers so they can find out more about their own potentials. They are looking for self-affirmation, either from within or from activities in which they can find success.

Another way older persons can like themselves is to admire how they look. Our face is the canvas on which our lives are painted. The *non*elderly do not yet have grey hair, and their faces are unlined. That signifies that they have not lived very much. A lined face means that the person has laughed more, cried more, worked harder, suffered, worried, and wondered more. It is a sign of maturity. Our package-oriented consumer society has tried to sell us the wrong kind of face. Having a face with lines on it means that the person has more wisdom, is more mature, is thus more beautiful. Maybe someday there will be a cosmetic that makes lines on young faces!

SUSAN

The next type of new-generation older person is called Susan, after Susan B. Anthony. Susans have found the joy of serving a cause that needs them. They find rejuvenating excitement in being involved in activities that they think are important. Although older persons can have the greatest impact on causes that do not affect them directly, such as child care for younger mothers or ecology, I am going to concentrate on a program that has direct benefits to older people as well. The program is "consciousness raising."

Consciousness raising has served a useful function for women and minority-group members. As long as women were seen by society as being too emotional and not capable of performing in some occupations, there was justification for sexism. As long as black people were perceived as lazy, shiftless, nonambitious, and inferior, there was no point in special programs for them. Both of these groups took on the characteristics attributed to them by society and this resulted in their having a lower level of self-esteem. Feeling less able, they performed poorly.

By instigating consciousness-raising programs, women and blacks changed their self-image and began seeing themselves as more capable. What we need to do now is learn from the success of these movements. I am proposing the establishment of agism studies centers. These need to be differentiated from centers for the study of aging, which focus on the current condition of the elderly and are not primarily concerned with changing images.

An agist-oriented program would have courses, public service, research, and advocacy programs. Some examples of possible consciousness-raising courses concern

1. Agism in the media with a special emphasis on TV. Watch TV and note how older persons are portrayed.

2. Agism in children's books. Are older persons perceived as functioning effectively outside the family?
3. Biographies of the elderly who have made significant contributions to various fields, such as music, art, philosophy, science, politics in their older years.
4. Discussion groups to discuss how agism has affected women, to raise their consciousness, and develop solidarity among them.
5. Biology of aging, to counteract some of the current myths about physical decline that can become self-fulfilling prophecies.
6. Contributions of older women to American society.
7. Consumer knowledge, so that we become aware, for example, why we have been sold this year the necessity of smelling like a lemon.
8. Financial management for the elderly, with special attention to increasing resources.
9. Contributions of the elderly in different historical periods—to American independence, the conquering of the West, in the Middle Ages.
10. Healthy personality among the elderly. It is possible that old age can be a time for a mature, self-actualized, creative, personality.
11. Geriadvocacy—study of the political process as it relates to the elderly. One suggestion is the organization of a League of Older Voters.

A major recommendation of this paper is that the Susans among the old push the professional centers for the study of aging into such social action as collating and distributing information about agism: course outlines, research projects in progress, ongoing programs of action against agism, and opportunities for participating in any of these projects. The centers need to be influenced in the direction of becoming more concerned with agism and consciousness raising among the elderly. Maggie Kuhn and the Gray Panthers movement represent a significant step in this direction.

As Neugarten (1968) points out, older persons are not a single type, but are characterized by diversity. The new generation of old women should not be limited by what others think they should be doing with their lives. Whether they are like Penelope, oriented around their husband; like Molly, involved with their children or grandchildren; like Narcissus, doing their own thing; or like Susan, arousing the world, is not the point. The question is whether they have made the existential choice of considering the here and now and finding meaning for themselves in one way or another.

I want to end with a little story. An adult asks a young teenager what she wants to be when she grows up. The teenager asks, "Do you mean when I really grow up?" When the reply is yes, she responds, "I want to be elderly. Elderly is beautiful and mature." If the elderly lead the way, they open up new worlds not only for themselves but for generations to come.

REFERENCES

Clavan, S., and E. Vatter, "The Affiliative Family in Non-Traditional Family Forms in the 70's," ed. Marvin Sussman. Minneapolis: National Council on Family Relations, 1973, pp. 131-136. Based on Two Groves Conference on the Family, 1971-72.

Deutscher, I., "The Quality of Postparental Life," *Journal of Marriage and the Family*, 26 (1964), 52-60.

Feldman, H., "The Effects of Children on the Family," in *Family Issues of Employed Women in Europe and America*, ed. Andrée Michel. Lieden, the Netherlands: E. F. Brill, 1971.

Feldman, H., and M. Feldman, "Marital Relationships during the Postparental Period," paper presented at the 26th Annual Meeting of the Institute of Gerontology, University of Michigan, Ann Arbor, September 10, 1973.

May, R., "Reaching Out for Inner Awareness, An Interview with Dr. Rollo May," *Ithaca in a Nutshell, A Handbook for College*, pp. 55-56, 1973.

Neugarten, B., *Middle Age and Aging*. Chicago: University of Chicago Press, 1968.

Osofsky, J., and E. O'Connell, "Parent-Child Interaction: Daughters' Effects upon Mothers' and Fathers' Behaviors," *Developmental Psychology*, 7, No. 2 (1972), 157-69.

Chapter 8

Coming Out of the Closet: Marriage and Other Crises of Middle Age

Florine B. Livson

Noel Coward's film *Brief Encounter* portrays a suburban English housewife approaching middle age as she confronts her disenchantment with her marriage and lifestyle. The film dramatizes a midlife crisis. It deals with the awakening of a woman—a middle-class wife and mother— to her lack of fulfillment in these roles and with her temptation to evolve a new life. She becomes aware of her alienation in her marriage through a brief romantic involvement with another man, and it is through him that she seeks redefinition and change. Her moral code, however, does not permit her to use the other man as a solution. In the end, she gives up her lover and reconfirms her commitment to her husband with the hope of new intimacy, though it is not clear how this intimacy is to be achieved, if at all. *Brief Encounter* was produced in 1946.[1]

Thirty years later another dramatist, Ingmar Bergman, portrays a different solution to a similar problem in his film, *Scenes from a Marriage.* An affluent, middle-class man and wife in middle adulthood—this time in Sweden—are introduced as a model couple successfully fulfilling their roles as husband, wife, and parents. Pro-

Florine B. Livson, Ph.D. is a psychologist at the Institute of Human Development, University of California, Berkeley. She is engaged in research on the transitions of adult life, particularly of middle age.

[1]The original play, aptly titled *Still Life,* was written in 1936.

gressively they reveal the superficiality of their relationship and their lack of intimacy. The marriage is disrupted when the husband abruptly leaves his wife for another woman. In this case, moral considerations do not stand in the way of the husband's move. Of greater interest, however, is the subsequent development of these two people. Both embark on a journey of self-discovery, adventuring into new roles and lifestyles. Each, in tandem with the other, alternates between living out childhood dreams and meeting adult disillusionment. Both discover fresh aspects of themselves in new relationships, even remarriage, but without fulfillment. Periodically they meet, only to discover they cannot reach one another, and separate again. It is only after each achieves some kind of individuation and self-acceptance that they are able to touch each other — if only briefly — with something like intimacy (significantly, outside the bonds of marriage).

Do these two dramas, written in different periods and social climates, reflect a shift in the values of our society, and in the institution of marriage itself? Both deal with disillusionment and alienation in the marital relationship as the protagonists approach middle age. Both, though set in different countries, reflect the values of middle-class, affluent members of industrial society. Yet Noel Coward's play affirms the preeminence of the marital institution over the individual. Bergman's drama places greater value on the individual. His film seems to assert that intimacy can be approached only when both partners have arrived at a separate sense of self, free of childhood dependencies and illustions; it also seems to say that marriage stifles this kind of self-realization.

To generalize this point of view: does marriage in some instances serve as a transitional stage in adult development — somewhere between childhood and full individuation of self — that has important functions in early adulthood but inhibits further development in middle life? Marriage in early adulthood may function as a kind of graduation ceremony, confirming the individual's separation from her or his family of origin. But at the same time it may be used to reconstitute the person's childhood roles. Earlier dependencies may be cast off, only to reappear in new clothing.

In this sense, the marital partner might be viewed as a transitional figure. That is, the spouse — particularly the husband but not always — may serve as a bridge between parental attachments and adult autonomy, or even as an invitation to regress to childhood roles. If so, and if the partners cannot move beyond this transitional stage within the marriage, they may, like Bergman's characters, choose to move out of the marriage to grow — particularly in middle life when aging itself may spark the urge to change.

Pressures to regress in marriage — to retreat into dependency or to inhibit individuality — are often greater for women than for men. Bernard (1973), in her extensive overview of the research literature, points to the general finding that wives make more of the adjustments in marriage than husbands and conform more to husbands' expectations than husbands do to wives'. She suggests that the "Pygmalion effect" of marriage results from the husband's role and not necessarily from his personal wishes or demands. During the early and middle years of marriage, husbands, as economic providers, continue to develop mastery skills (assertiveness, independence, competence) that build self-esteem. Wives, more concerned with their performance in familial roles, may define themselves through their relationships with others and lose ground in their development as self- directing adults.

Blake traces the evolution of women's secondary economic (and social) status in industrialized nations:

> The migration of industrializing peoples out of rural settings into urban factories and bureaucracies . . . progressively removed work from the family milieu and put men in jobs away from home. . . . Gradually, both wives and children became economic liabilities to the men. . . . Industrializing societies [developed] all kinds of rationalizations and legitimations for the wrenching change in the position of women that was accompanying the Industrial Revolution and the demographic transition. In particular they [asserted] that women's personalities and behavior actually conformed by nature to the restrictions of their new way of life. (1974, p. 92)

Thus our society socializes women to adopt a self-image that fits their secondary economic status. Wives are encouraged to assume a complementary role to their husband's assertiveness by suppressing (or at least masking) their own competitiveness and power drives. Many women respond by seeking out the Pygmalion in their husbands. They project power and competence onto men. As a result, conflicts and anxieties over assuming adult roles in the larger society can be postponed, sometimes indefinitely. The woman may resent her dependency while gaining security from it—and feel helpless to modify either. A woman who divorces later in life or who is widowed may again be confronted with issues of typical adolescence: developing independence and an identity apart from her family.

However, the institution of marriage in our society seems to be changing. The divorce rate in this country has been rising steadily since 1962.[2] Between 1962 and 1974, the divorce rate more than doubled (from 2.2 to 4.6 per 1,000 population), with the sharpest rate of increase from 1973 to 1974 (4.4 to 4.6 per 1,000). Most demographers point out, however, that this should not be taken as evidence that the marital institution is falling into disfavor. "Only a trivial proportion of people eschew marriage altogether, and approximately 80 percent of those who . . . divorce remarry" (Ryder, 1974, p. 87). The statistics do suggest that serial monogamy has become an alternate pattern of marriage in our society.

Though most divorces occur during the first years of marriage, older people are divorcing more too. From 1963 to 1969, divorces among women 55 years and older increased by over 34 percent. Six percent of all divorces in 1969 involved couples who had been married for twenty-five years or more.

The middle years of marriage, when children reach their teens and begin to separate, are often stressful. Studies of changes in marital happiness over the life course suggest that satisfaction drops to a low point during this stage of family life. (However, for couples who do not divorce, happiness increases after the children leave [Deutscher, 1964; Pineo, 1961; Rollins and Feldman, 1970].)

Changes in the permanence of marriage have been linked by various writers to changes in the institution of the family itself in urban, post-industrial society. Divorce rates have been rising not only in the United States but in most developed countries. Ryder (1974), among others, observes that the family has lost most of the functions it had in traditional society except for emotional bonding. Its function as an economic unit (on family farms and in small businesses or, in pre-industrial society, in cottage industries) has almost disappeared. Even parenting—a traditional cornerstone of family life—is shared more and more with outside institutions.

[2]Demographic data are taken from the U.S. Bureau of the Census unless otherwise indicated.

Rapid changes in social values and in technical skills widen the generation gap, making it difficult for parents to be adequate models for their children. Schools, peer groups, and, to an extent, the mass media have replaced some of the traditional authority of parents. The bond between spouses too is weakened by modern technology; with more efficient birth control, husbands and wives are no longer held together by sexual exclusiveness. These and other social changes—for example, greater mobility—have eroded family cohesiveness and added to family strain.

The rising divorce rate, however, may reflect not so much increased marital unhappiness as the ease with which marital unhappiness can now be terminated. Divorce laws have become more liberal. Religious views sanctifying monogamy "till death do us part" are changing. A new morality is on the upswing. This morality urges people to change. It places individual fulfillment above obligation to others as a desirable goal. It exhorts women and men to shake free of traditional commitments and to adopt new lifestyles, in and out of marriage. This ethic is reflected in various social movements that have gained momentum in recent years: the sexual revolution, the personal growth movement, and, not least, the women's movement.

In the past decade, more and more Americans, especially from the educated middle class, have turned to the pursuit of personal growth. Organizations promoting fulfillment through change sponsor countless weekend seminars and summer retreats. Developing one's potential has become a major leisure activity for many Americans—and a profitable industry. The American dream of infinite growth, once applied to economic expansion, has been translated into personal growth. And the ideal of individualism, always a strong value in American politics and business, has been applied to self-fulfillment.

These goals have become a major platform of the feminist movement. Women are urged to assert their individuality rather than to live for and through others. Housewives are encouraged to find an identity apart from their husbands—to develop their potential as separate and equal adults. Women's groups, women's magazines, and television all call upon women to reevaluate their lifestyles, to define themselves by other than domestic roles.

Are women responding to this call? One sign that the American housewife has been moving out of the house for some time is a striking increase over the past two decades in the number of married women in the United States who hold paying jobs. In 1950, less than 25 percent of married women aged 15 to 64 were working; in 1970 over 40 percent were working (Blake, 1974). Not surprisingly, this increase goes along with a widespread change in values. Blake reports that a 1945 Gallup survey found that only 18 percent of the population approved of a married woman working. By 1973, 65 percent approved when the same question was asked. Clearly, it has become more acceptable for a married woman to work and more married women are doing so. Though many work to supplement the family income and few have jobs that pay them as well as men are paid, the economic position of women has become less dependent than a generation ago.

Not only on the economic scene but with respect to their marriages, women are coming out of the closet. Holding themselves less responsible for succeeding in marriage— indeed, feeling less pressure to be married—women are freer to disclose negative feelings about their marriages. They are sharing responsibility for marital success more equally with their husbands. To fail in marriage, though probably still a source of shame or guilt for many women, is losing its sting for many others—and for some is coming to be redefined as a step toward liberation or growth.

Several women in their 40s meeting regularly in a women's discussion group, for example, discovered that each had kept feelings of dissatisfaction in their marriages secret for years out of loyalty to their husbands and families. This protective attitude masked a sense of responsibility and personal failure. Some had kept such feelings hidden even from themselves, paying the price of tension and depression. One woman confessed she realized she was unhappy in her marriage only after she had returned to college to pursue a new career. In retrospect, she saw that returning to school had been her way of moving out of her marriage; ultimately, she obtained a divorce.

This shift in women's social conscience has not, of course, spread equally to all segments of the population; and its impact is only beginning to be felt, even where the push to change is strongest. Changes in social institutions in this country tend to spread from the East and West Coasts to the middle areas and from urban to suburban communities. They filter from upper-middle to middle and then to lower socioeconomic strata with wide differences in ethnic groups and age. (A larger proportion of black than white women in this country, for example, are divorced or separated.[3]) Therefore, in this and the following sections, keep in mind that I am referring to middle-class, white women who, roughly defined, are part of urban culture.

The generation of women now reaching middle age bears the brunt of this shift in social values. Most began their married lives in the decade following World War II. This was the decade when the feminine mystique was at its height (see Bernard, 1973). Idealized visions of family life dominated the value scene. Women were super-homebodies and super-mothers. The birthrate, which had been gradually declining throughout this century, rose between 1947 and 1957. Women were having larger families than any generation born since 1890, and they were beginning them sooner after marriage than at any time in the twentieth century. They were leaving college earlier to marry earlier. They validated their worth by embracing traditional feminine roles — marriage, mothering, and the domestic arts — in, one suspects, a kind of frantic denial of secular ambition or, at least, a sublimation of drives toward achievement. Women who deviated were devalued. Working mothers met with disapproval and career women were suspected of neurotic competition with men. (Various reasons have been proposed for this revivial of traditional femininity, ranging from a reaction to the interruption of family life during the war years to the influence of Freudian thinking.)

This generation of women, now in their late 40s and early 50s, are confronted by an about-face in the values to which they were socialized as young adults. The new values present new opportunities — but may also cause pressure and conflict. Feminist ideology and alternative lifestyles available to young women question the lifestyles and values of older women — especially at a time of transition and choice in their own lives. Some (possibly most) respond by rejecting liberated values and reaffirming the traditional roles to which they have been committed. Others reach out to the expanded opportunities now available to women, joining the growing number of middle-aged women reentering the educational system and the work force. The number of women in the labor market rises sharply among women between ages 45 and 54; over half of all women in this age group are gainfully employed

---

[3]U.S. Bureau of the Census, 1972, Table 1.

(Neugarten, 1970). Women (and men) of all ages are also enrolling in community schools and colleges in increasing numbers. Some colleges and universities now have special programs for older adults, a few geared mainly to women. Some middle-aged women, however, find satisfaction neither in traditional lifestyles nor alternative roles. They may suffer from feelings of deprivation or inadequacy or envy of the young (including sometimes their children) or from a vague sense of discontent and bewilderment. The classical problems of middle age can be complicated by this swing in the social pendulum over the course of one generation.

The middle years of the adult life span—particularly the decade between ages 40 and 50—are a time of transition and reevaluation, heightened for women by the departure of children and by the biological changes of menopause and its psychological implications. Neugarten and Moore, analyzing changes from 1890 to 1966 in the ages at which women in this country marry, have children, and participate in the labor force, find "an [earlier and] increasingly accentuated transition period in the lives of women" (1968, p. 13). A few generations ago, with larger families and children spaced further apart, the last child married when women were, on the average, 55 years old. Today this occurs at 47. This is the age, they point out, when the number of women on the labor market rises abruptly and also the average age at menopause, according to most medical literature.

The emergence of the postparental years as a significant phase in a woman's life is a relatively new social phenomenon. With increased longevity—today a woman of 45 will live on the average 33 more years—and the earlier departure of children, a woman can now expect a longer period without her children and, ultimately, without her husband. (The majority of women over 65 are widowed.) Thus, the departure of children brings about an important change in a woman's life, comparable in some ways to occupational retirement in men. In both, a major role contributing to the individual's identity is lost. But the average woman retires from mothering with two-fifths of her life left to live. Her grown children (and grandchildren) are likely to move to other communities and to be preoccupied with their own lives. Most women must look elsewhere for satisfaction in the second half of life.

However, several studies—Neugarten (1970) and Lowenthal, Thurnher, and Chiriboga (1975), to cite two—have found that the major crisis of middle age for women occurs when the departure of children is anticipated but not yet realized. (This is also when a woman is apt to be coping with the ups and downs of adolescent children in their struggle for psychological separation.) The study by Lowenthal et al. finds that women at this life stage are under considerable stress, generally dissatisfied with themselves and their marriages, and pessimistic about the future. Both studies, however, find that life satisfaction improves in the postparental period when children have actually departed. Neugarten also reports that menopause is a more benign event in the lives of middle-aged women than is commonly believed. Neugarten observes that these findings do not deny that major role changes at middle age may be experienced as losses, but they do suggest that when role changes are expected and occur "on schedule" in the normal life course, they can be anticipated and worked through without disrupting the woman's sense of self.

But the psychological impact of becoming middle-aged is not limited to coping with changes in cultural values or to menopause or marriage or even to loss of the mothering role. Awareness of aging, of entering the second half of life, is itself a potent force that may lead to reevaluation and to changes in lifestyle. Women and men become aware of themselves as temporal beings. The sense of timelessness enjoyed in youth may be replaced by a new urgency and an awareness of missed experience, or by relief in settling for what is. Either way, there may be an increased need to plan and take responsibility for the future before time runs out. Defenses of denial and procrastination ("Someday I'll do it," "When the kids grow up," "When I have time," etc.) are less effective.

Along with this shift in the sense of time, there is often a heightened consciousness of self, comparable to the adolescent years. Issues of identity—of who one is and where one is going and whether one is satisfied with one's lifestyle—become prominent. Not only the conflicts of adolescence but the sense of excitement and hope may be revived. This tendency to look inward and forward can lead to enlightened planning, to experimenting with changes in lifestyle. Or, when anxiety is the prime motivator, individuals may act impulsively, making abrupt and sometimes destructive changes in their lives. Some middle-aged divorces undoubtedly fall into this category. Others do not. Increased freedom to choose alternative lifestyles can lead to growth and enrichment. But questioning one's commitment to traditional roles can also evoke anxiety and conflict.

Both sexes in our youth-oriented society tend to be concerned with physiological decline in later life. Men at middle age may fear loss of sexual potency or impaired vigor and health. But physiological aging poses special problems for women. Growing old strikes at the core of a woman's pride. Sontag (1972), in a strong polemic against the "double standard of aging" for men and women in our culture, calls attention to the damaging effects of aging on a woman's desirability and sense of worth. Insofar as women are valued for beauty and female beauty is equated with youth, aging robs a woman of her main value and her self-esteem. Though this "obsolescence" occurs later than it used to (with better health, hormones, cosmetics), the pattern remains unchanged.

Men, Sontag observes, are permitted two standards of physical attractiveness—the youth and the man. Women are permitted only one. A man's sexual attractiveness is enhanced by signs of aging—thickening of the body, lines on the face, graying hair. Furthermore, his desirability is enhanced by what he does—by power, wealth, achievement—which increases with age. Similarly, while older men receive social approval for marrying or consorting with younger women, women receive less approval—are even criticized—for dating or marrying younger men. Thus, older women who are divorced or widowed are usually less likely to find suitable marriage partners than are older men.

Sontag suggests that this double standard is rooted in a deep-seated fear of women in this culture, split into admiration for the girl and distaste for the old woman. To the degree that women share these values with men (and often they do), signs of aging can lead to self-hate. Sontag views the double standard of aging as an example of male privilege to which women acquiesce by retreating from adult roles—for example, by assigning men the initiative for courtship. She makes a plea for women to assume adult roles earlier in life, to continue them longer, and to "allow their faces to show the lives they have lived."

Not all women, of course, respond the same way to becoming middle-aged. Neugarten (1970), in a study of 100 wives and mothers aged 43 to 53, found no relationship between psychological well-being and changes in lifestyle during this age period. How a particular woman experiences herself at this time of life and how she adapts to the many social and psychological forces impinging on her will depend, to a large degree, on her personality—on the strengths and sensitivities she brings to the situation— and on the unique circumstances of her life. The key factor may be the "fit" between a woman's personality and her social roles.

This view is supported by a recent study in which I followed the personality development of a group of psychologically healthy middle-aged women who had been observed periodically since adolescence (Livson, 1974).[4] All were white, middle-class housewives and mothers, though some also worked. I identified two types of women functioning successfully by age 50. Both had evolved stable personality styles by adolescence that remained consistent over time, but each followed a different path leading to psychological health at age 50.

One group, "traditionals," were conventional, sociable, nurturing women at 50 who valued intimacy; they were "feminine" in the traditional sense. Their personal style, congruent with their roles as wives and mothers, showed steady growth over the life span. They moved smoothly into middle age, continuing to find satisfaction in interpersonal relationships, even as their children grew older and left home. A second group, "independents," were, at 50, intellectual, achievement-oriented, and unconventional. From adolescence on, they were "doers" rather than "socializers." With personalities less suited to domestic roles, independents experienced a crisis in early adulthood. By 40, they were depressed and irritable, out of touch with their intellectual and creative potential. By age 50, however, this crisis was resolved. Disengaging from the mothering role when their children left home, they revived their intellectual interests and picked up the threads of their earlier ambition, with a corresponding freeing of emotional expression.

Thus for women whose personalities fit a conventional orientation, traditional roles are not particularly restricting. For women who are less conventionally feminine — who prefer to deal with life in modes usually defined as masculine — traditional roles can be restricting. But middle age can bring new opportunities for growth.

As this study suggests, women would do well to wear the roles that fit them. Not all personalities are suited to the same lifestyle. But relatively few women — especially in older age groups — have been socialized to choose roles that are tailored to their individual style. Most continue to follow more or less conventional paths in spite of changing social stereotypes and expanding (though still

[4]These women are part of an ongoing longitudinal study at the Institute of Human Development, University of California, Berkeley.

limited) options. The middle-aged woman today, however, has more alternatives available to her than a generation ago — and more social pressure to change. Middle age now offers a second chance to a generation of women conditioned to live traditional lives. But the current generation of young women are in an even better position to arrange their lives in accord with their personal style. Perhaps, unlike the characters in Bergman's film, they need not wait for middle age to reach toward their full potential.

REFERENCES

Bernard, J., *The Future of Marriage.* New York: Bantam Books, Inc., 1973.

Blake, J., "The Changing Status of Women in Developed Countries," in *The Human Population* (A Scientific-American Book). San Francisco: W. H. Freeman, 1974.

Deutscher, I., "The Quality of Postparental Life," *Journal of Marriage and the Family*, 26, No. 1 (1964), 52–60.

Livson, F. B., "Evolution of Self: Personality Development in Middle-Aged Women," doctoral dissertation, The Wright Institute, 1974. *Dissertation Abstracts International*, 36, No. 2 (1975) (University Microfilms No. 75-16, 963)

Lowenthal, M. F., M. Thurnher, and D. Chiriboga, *Four Stages of Life.* San Francisco: Jossey-Bass, 1975.

Neugarten, B. L., "Adaptation and the Life Cycle," *Journal of Geriatric Psychiatry*, 4 (1970), 71–87.

Neugarten, B. L., and J. W. Moore, "The Changing Age-Status System," in *Middle Age and Aging: A Reader in Social Psychology*, ed. B. L. Neugarten. Chicago: University of Chicago Press, 1968.

Pineo, P. C., "Disenchantment in the Later Years of Marriage," *Marriage and Family Living*, 23 (1961), 3–11.

Rollins, B. C., and H. Feldman, "Marital Satisfaction Over the Family Life Cycle," *Journal of Marriage and the Family*, 32, No. 1 (1970), 20–28.

Ryder, N. B., "The Family in Developed Countries," in *The Human Population* (A Scientific-American Book). San Francisco: W. H. Freeman, 1974.

Sontag, S., "The Double Standard of Aging," *Saturday Review of the Society*, October 1972, pp. 29–38.

Chapter 9

The Meaning of Friendship
in Widowhood

Helena Znaniecki Lopata

Americans are confused about friendship. We have idealized it, yet we view it with caution, even with fear. We conjure images of fraternal (more often than sororal) bonds, of "buddy" comradeship, of the sharing of intimate secrets, and of perfect symmetry of commitment between people equal in power and status (Little, 1970; Lowenthal and Haven, 1968). This equality is supposed to be reinforced by similarity of background and a sharing of values. Friends are supposed to be willing to sacrifice everything, even their lives, for each other and to put their friendship ahead of all other relationships. At the same time, we don't think our own lives can contain such deep relationship because there are other roles we must perform. We may feel that we once had such a friendship, maybe even more than one, when we were young — and we may hope that we can have it again in the future, when we have time for it.

We suspect that friendship, in its ideal form, could lead to

Helena Znaniecki Lopata is a professor of sociology and director of the Center for the Comparative Study of Social Roles, Loyola University of Chicago. The study of the "support systems of widows in an urbanized area of America" was funded through a contract with the Social Security Administration (Contract # SSA 71-3411). The stratified sample was drawn from lists of widows presently receiving benefits because of being mothers of dependent children or having reached the age of 60 or 62 and of widows who are former beneficiaries, now remarried, with adult children or recipients of only the "lump-sum" payment to help cover funeral costs.

disloyalty to family or employer. Although we spend millions of dollars in learning "How to Win Friends and Influence People" (Carnegie, 1936), we worry about the consequences of friendship among adults. Cross-sex intimacy is presumed to inevitably lead to sexual intercourse. Same-sex friendships for either man or woman are seen as potentially interfering with the marital bond. Since husbands and wives are considered perfect companions, neither should need another close friend. Women must "hang loose" in their relationships so as not to interfere with their husband's career and their shared social life. A wife must be ready to move, leaving friends behind, when her husband's job calls for a transfer or when his success calls for a new lifestyle and new associates with which to share it. Old friends are at a distance, not just geographically, but socially. Husbands must be ready to move up to the next rung on occupational ladders and must not develop close ties at work that need to be broken (Whyte, 1956). They must also be careful whom they associate with away from the job. Above all, it is dangerous to exchange confidences—people may use these against you. Wives also must watch what they say and to whom they say it so as not to endanger their husband's breadwinning responsibility.

Many of these attitudes toward friendship arose within the last two centuries in Western Europe and the last few decades in America, as the family became privatized and isolated from the general life of the society (Aries, 1962). In fact, all personal social relations were pushed into the background as the Protestant Ethic (Weber, 1930) and its puritanical embellishment in America focused on the economic sphere of life (Dulles, 1965). America grew dramatically in affluence and complexity because of this push toward industrialization, technology, and capitalism, and work became organized into a myriad of occupations carried out by the marital team with the husband as the main breadwinner on the job and the wife as the maintainer of the home and family.

Involvement in the community and economic life of both women and men changed dramatically: wives became restricted to the home with only sporadic contacts with relatives, neighbors, and other friends, and husbands focused their identity, time, and energy almost exclusively on their occupational roles. Even after it became common for women to work outside the home before they married, or at least before the birth of their first child, and even when married women went back to jobs after raising children, their primary commitment was to the home. Few women took their roles outside the home seriously. The economic growth of American society demanded a willingness to push aside relationships which could interfere with work. Husband-wife, parent-child, kin, friendship, and neighboring relations seem, as a result, to have suffered from these changes and the predominance given to the economic value system.

Only in one group in our society has friendship been fully encouraged: in older people. They are no longer supposed to be involved in the basic roles of breadwinner and wife of breadwinner and are freed from worry over the dangers friendship could impose on their lives. The older woman is free from the obligation to have and care for children and, if her husband dies, even from her role of wife. Her husband, if he survives till retirement, need no longer worry about developing disadvantageous alliances or about disclosure of infomation that could hurt his job or career. Old men and women are supposed to be less interested in sex, so even cross-sex friendships are permissible.

Of course, the encouragement of friendship among older Americans may not necessarily lead to their formation, at least in their idealized form (Blau, 1961, 1973). In order to determine the actual importance of friendship in the lives of older Americans, we can examine the way it fits in the support systems of urban widows. A support system includes the exchange of an action or an object which the giver and/or receiver defines as necessary or helpful in maintaining a style of life. Each person is involved in various forms of support exchanges, financial, service, social, or emotional (Lopata, 1975 a).

FRIENDSHIP IN WIDOWHOOD

In order to learn the importance of friendship in the lives of women who no longer have to be devoted either to the role of wife or mother, we studied over 1,000 widows living in the Chicago area. These women represented over 82,000 widows who were or had recently been beneficiaries of social security. We can predict two opposite possibilities. On the one hand, these widows might become heavily oriented toward friendship, both deepening relations with old friends and developing new friends. They might engage in a variety of social activities, turning to others for emotional and even service supports. On the other hand, these women might be more apt to follow the personality and lifestyle habits of their past, so that those widows who had relied little on friends in the past would not change into becoming friend-oriented when their roles of wife and mother decreased in importance. People tend to develop a style of dealing with the world that continues throughout life, albeit with modifications introduced by changing definitions or circumstances. Thus, in spite of the fact that widows are free to make their own friendships, it is quite possible that they will follow the pattern they developed while the husband was still living. What they do with their friends, how much time they spend with them, and even whom they are friendly with might change with widowhood, but women who have been strongly involved in friendship relations will probably continue to be so involved and the friendless will continue being friendless. Conditions such as education, income, and race can be expected to affect friendship now as they did when the women were married (Lopata, 1973a, 1973b, 1975b). We can expect widows to be friends mostly with other widows (Lopata, 1973a; Rosow, 1967; Blau, 1973; Lowenthal, 1968). Strains could develop in relations with people who are still married. Widows have more in common with other widows, and have little opportunity to retain the style of social life that is based on couples (Cumming and Henry, 1961). Finally, we can expect that close personal friends will appear as service, social, and emotional supports of widows.

The life-pattern expectations of friendships are supported by our widowhood study. Very few of those widows who said they had no friends the year before their husband's fatal illness or accident developed new friendships after he died. Over one-third of the women kept their old friends but did not develop new ones. Another third said they have both old and new friends. This leaves a surprising one-sixth of the widows who claimed to be totally without friends both when their husband was still well and at the time of the study.

THE FRIENDLESS WIDOW

The completely friendless women were most apt to have been born outside Chicago, migrating from another country or from American rural areas. An even larger porportion had nonurban parents. Proportionately more black than white widows claimed to have no close friends, and there was found to be a strong association between the number of years of formal education and not only whether they had friends but also how many. The amount of formal schooling affected whom they married, their husband's background, and the jobs he could obtain during his lifetime. The job, in turn, affected family income and lifestyle. Furthermore, the older the women, the more likely they were to have suffered a double burden. They were likely to have been immersed in a culture suspicious of nonrelative "strangers," one that viewed the world as an unfriendly place. They were also likely to have lived a lifestyle that provided little time, energy, or money for leisure-time pursuits or had the advantages of a society of abundance that make pleasurable friendship possible (Znaniecki, 1965, Lopata, 1969, 1971, 1973a, 1973b). They are now living in a situation in which the traditional support systems of family and neighborhood have dissolved, yet they are unaccustomed to going out to look for and develop new social relations and social roles. They either never develop social networks outside the family, or they cannot reengage in society once former networks are disorganized by death, the dispersal of siblings or children, or financial or health changes. These are the more isolated women. Their lives were peripheral to the modern urban social world even when the husband was living. They are even more isolated after his death.

The friendless women do not necessarily say they want friends. They are likely to believe that "relatives are your only true friends" (Lopata, 1973a, 1975b). Over half of these widows in the recent study who claimed they had no personal friends when their husband was alive and none since his death disagree with the statement "I wish I had more friends." Nor does the absence of friends automatically lead to dissatisfaction with life or loneliness. When asked to define their level of loneliness in comparison to what they assume is true of other people, over half place themselves as "less lonely than most people," "rarely" or "never" lonely. Since loneliness is often a matter of relative deprivation, in that the person experiencing it compared her or his level of social interaction to a higher level experienced in the past or assumed to be experienced by others, we are led to believe that these women do not expect social interaction with people identified as friends (Lopata, 1969, 1973b; Weiss, 1973).

There seem to be two types of friendless widows (probably

friendless people in general). One type does not identify friendship as part of life, does not expect to have friends, and is not lonely or dissatisfied with life in their absence, The other type wants friends and is lonely and dissatisfied with life. This second type is apt to lack the self-confidence, the "aggressive" initiative, or the knowledge of procedures needed to venture out of her environment, even after it becomes disorganized by the death of her husband. Such a widow is likely to sit at home passively, waiting for someone else to initiate contacts and interaction. Unfortunately, there are few people who have the time or inclination to go through the laborious process of converting such a woman into a socially involved person. People similar to her, who could become friends because of similarity, also lack the resources for doing so. There are undoubtedly many women who are not widows who have the same lack of personal resources for building social networks.

THE WOMAN WITH PRE-WIDOWHOOD FRIENDS

By contrast, women who stated that they had close personal friends the year before their husband's death, and especially those who listed more than one such intimate, were found to be younger, both at the time of the study and the time of widowhood, to be better educated, with higher incomes when their husband was living and also at the time of the study, and to be white. They themselves were apt to have been working just before or during widowhood and to have held white-collar jobs. Their late husband was also most likely to have been in a white-collar occupation.

Three-fourths of all the widows listed at least one friend before their husband's fatal illness or accident, with an average of almost three per person. Most of these friends were women, but men were sometimes mentioned, usually as part of a couple. Couple friendship is characteristic of the American middle class, whose social life is, in fact, embedded in couple- companionate leisure-time interaction (Znaniecki, 1965; Lopata, 1971, 1973a, 1975b). Widows seldom listed a man without his wife, again reflecting the traditional discouragement of individualized cross-sex friendship.

Most of the pre-widowhood friendships mentioned were longstanding, known for more than ten years before the husband's death. Almost all of the people were married at that time, which supports the couple-companionate thesis (Hunt, 1966; Blau, 1973). Contrary to the findings of earlier studies of friendship among couples (Babchuk, 1965; Babchuk and Bates, 1963), in which the husband was said to have selected the couples they were friends with, the Chicago-area widows took the credit for developing their couple friendships. They said they did so by taking advantage of contacts in their neighborhood, through voluntary associations, or at work. Sometimes they found friends through relatives or even more esoteric places such as bars or doctor's offices. Younger women were still likely to have friends from childhood.

Most of the pre-widowhood friends were seen an average of once a week, though there were racial and educational differences. The more socially involved women, who had more friends, often had a lower average frequency of contact with their friends when their husband was still alive. However, few of the widows were able to maintain the same frequency of contact with their old friends. At least, by the time they were being interviewed, the frequency had dropped to "several times a year," although most old friends were still considered friends. Changed circumstances of life often make contact difficult, but a major problem, particularly among the middle-class women accustomed to couple-companionate interaction, is the asymmetry produced by a husband's death. Widows report feeling like a "fifth wheel" when they try to go out with, or go to the home of couple friends unless they "have a date" (Lopata, 1973a, 1975a). To make matters worse, new widows are not only husbandless and even escortless, but they are apt to be grieving, which makes friends feel awkward and uncomfortable. Their friends complain that they do not respond to friendly advances, the relations become strained, the widows' lowered self-confidence makes them oversensitive, and they drift apart. Whoever is at fault, contacts with married friends were found to decrease, particularly when the husbands were present.

Friends who were not tied to a couple-companionate round of activities were found to be more easily retained in widowhood. Of course, some of these old friends had themselves become widowed, in which case contact often increased. The widows who reported themselves as the "most lonely person" they know or "more lonely than most people" had experienced a dramatic drop in contacts with old friends and an inability to replace them with new friends. Thus, the most lonely were the women who lost not just a husband but also friends from the past, both in terms of closeness and in frequency of interactions.

THE WOMAN WITH POST-WIDOWHOOD FRIENDS

Over half of the widows in the study claimed they had not made new friends since their husband died. Again, there was found to be a strong association between education and the making of new friends. The more educated developed more friends. Current total household income proved to be a greater influence on the ability to develop new friendships than did prior income, partly because many widows experienced a considerable drop of income with the death of their husband. It was reported that new friends were also met primarily in the neighborhood, through voluntary associations, or on the job—the same sources of contacts before widowhood. Most of these new friends were married, mainly because most women in the younger age groups are still in that marital status, but there were many more who were widowed. There was also a strong increase in men listed without a wife and some men were even identified as "boyfriends." A few of the widows in the study have already remarried.

CONTRIBUTIONS OF FRIENDS
TO THE SUPPORT SYSTEMS OF WIDOWS

Generally speaking, those women who listed old friends or developed new friends found them helpful during the time when they were rebuilding their lives following the death of their husband and the heavy grief period. Only one-tenth of the widows with friends evaluated them as rarely or never helpful. In fact, friends were judged as helpful during this traumatic time of life more often than any other significant associates except adult children.

In view of the frequency with which these widows listed friends, particularly old friends, as very helpful during the time they were rebuilding their life, it is surprising to find that friends did not appear as frequent contributors to their support systems. We listed about sixty-five different economic, service, emotional, and social supports, giving each woman the opportunity to name three persons for each support. This means that the widow could have listed as many as 195 names, although she could give the same person in several different supports. The list included emotional supports the year before the husband's death as well as at the time of the study. Economic and service supports being examined included both an in-flow, with the widow as the recipient, and an out-flow, with her as the giver. The social supports asked about specified social activities which people often share with others.

Friends were almost totally absent from the list of people providing economic supports, as givers or receivers of money or gifts; as helpers in payment of rent, food, or clothing; or as helpers in meeting other bills. In fact, the widows were relatively financially independent. Friends were also relatively absent from service supports such as helping with household repairs, shopping, housekeeping, yard work, child care, car care, decision making, legal aid, or transportation.

Friends did appear, however, in the social support system. We can conclude from this that if widows engage at all in typical urban American social activities, they often do so with people listed as friends. Although half of our population does not go to public places like movie theaters, over one-third of those who do, go with a friend. Again, although one-fifth of the widows claimed never to visit anyone, four in ten of those visited were friends. They were the people whom the widows were most likely to entertain or share lunches with. Playing cards or engaging in sports or other games is also a friend-sharing activity; over half of the companions listed for these activities were friends. It must be noted, however, that over half of the women in the study had never engaged in such activities. On the other hand, friends were found to be much less likely to be companions in church attendance, in travel out-of- town, or in celebrating holidays. All in all, many women appeared to be remarkably restricted in their social activities. Polite companionship (Znaniecki, 1965) and interaction which Americans supposedly engage in during their leisure time (Dulles, 1965) does not seem to describe the social life of many widows, particularly the older ones with less education and more of a blue-collar lifestyle.

In spite of the relative prominence of friends in the social support system of socially active widows, they were found to be largely absent in the emotional support system. Less than one in ten of the people named as those the women felt closest to the year before their husband's death were friends. Almost one in four named their husband as the person they had felt closest to, and a third named their children. Moreover, their husband's death did not push many of them toward friends. Only one-tenth of "closest" references for the time of the study were listed as friends. The same distribution occurred when we asked the widow whom she most enjoyed being with when her husband was well and whom she most enjoyed being with at the time the study was conducted. A friend was not even the main confidante for most widows. About one-tenth said that they told their problems to a friend, either before widowhood or now. Even fewer women said they turned to their friends for comfort when they were feeling blue or for help in times of crises. Few got the feeling of being an important person from their friends. At the same time, few said friends were the people they were most often angry at. When the researchers asked, "Now I am going to read some 'feeling states' which many people think are important for a full life. What persons or groups made (make) you feel this way in 19__ (the year before the late husband's death)/now?" Few women mentioned friends. The feeling of being "respected" drew less than a tenth of references to friends now and an even smaller proportion for the "before" period; the feelings of being "useful," "independent," "self- sufficient," or "secure" drew very few friends for the "before" and just a little bit more for the "now" period. Only the feeling of being "accepted" drew more than one- tenth of the references. Most women who turned to friends to meet emotional needs did so only after having listed someone else, usually their husband when he was alive and their children now. Children rather than friends are looked to for most emotional supports.

SUMMARY AND CONCLUSIONS

However idealized friendship is in American society and however women are assumed to turn to friendship when they are freed from the obligations and involvements of their basic roles of wife and mother, most Chicago-area widows were not found to follow this pattern. Although some women in the study were deeply involved in their relations with friends, the surprising finding of the widowhood study was that so few were. Some widows appeared to be socially isolated. They had no friends before their husband's death and they have no friends when they are widows. Other women had a limited number of friends, almost invariably other women, when their husband was living and they were able to bring these sex-segregated friendships into widowhood. There were widows who reflected the style of life described by Whyte (1956), in which most social relations are built around the man's job and career. They tended to associate almost exclusively with other couples and engaged in couple-companionate interaction, usually during evenings and especially weekends. These women had difficulties maintaining such friendships into widowhood. Being the "fifth wheel" on social occasions, often feeling an unwillingness on the part of married women friends to include them, they were left out of that type of interaction. They then found that they had to convert their social life into sharing lunches or other activities that women engage in during the absence of men and remain alone during the times that call for couple sharing. Other widows, usually the younger ones, obtained escorts or even new husbands and rejoined old groups or formed a new couple-companionate circle.

The social superficiality of relations considered "close friendships" emerges when we try to determine if people listed as friends are actually involved in the support systems of wives and later, widows. It is here we see that undertaking social activities with old or new friends does not convert itself into deeper involvement in the economic, service, or even emotional support systems. When given a chance to list as many as three persons closest to her, to whom she tells problems and who comfort her when she is blue, nine-tenths of the Chicago area widows did not even think of the friends they had listed as "close personal friends." Apparently, Americans' cautious attitudes about friends prevent even widows from forming close relations with them.

However, the distribution of friendship within our population of widows leads to some predictions as to this relationship in the future. Friendships were shown to be least frequent, and least deeply involving, among the least educated and the most disadvantaged of the Chicago-area women. The more white-collar women, even those near the border of poverty in widowhood, wished for friendships and had the personal resources for developing them. Thus, the blue-collar or working-class ideology that identifies relatives as the only possible friends for women, as well as customs that have no place for procedures to convert strangers into social companions, seem to restrict friendships of women more than does the middle-class ideology that cautions women to avoid strong friendships because of their husband's career. Should present middle-class values predominate, we can expect to find more true friendships among women, married or not. This does not solve the problems of the widow, accustomed to couple interaction and now deprived of the escort needed to engage in it. Nor does it guarantee friendship involvement beyond social support systems. If the feminist movement increases its influence down through the American class system, we can expect, however, that women will get greater satisfaction from friendship with other women, and that widows will feel less stigma from being husbandless. Feminism may also lead to greater depth in woman-to-woman relationships.

REFERENCES

Aries, Philippe, Centuries of Childhood. New York: Vintage Books, 1962.

Babchuk, Nicholas, "Primary Friends and Kin: A Study of the Associations of Middle-Class Couples," Social Forces (1965), pp. 483-93.

Babchuk, Nicholas, with A. P. Bates, "Primary Relations of Middle-Class Couples: A Study of Male Dominance," American Sociological Review, 28 (1963), 374-84.

Blau, Zena, "Structural Constraints of Friendship in Old Age," American Sociological Review, 26 (1961), 429-39.

_____, Old Age in a Changing Society. New York: Franklin Watts, 1973.

Carnegie, Dale, How to Win Friends and Influence People. New York: Simon & Schuster, 1936.

Cumming, Elaine, and William E. Henry, Growing Old: The Process of Disengagement. New York: Basic Books, 1961.

Dulles, Foster Rhea, A History of Recreation. New York: Appleton-Century-Crofts, 1965.

Hunt, Morton M., The World of the Formerly Married. New York: McGraw-Hill, 1966.

Little, Roger, "Buddy Relations and Combat Performance," in The Sociology of Organizations: Basic Studies, ed. Oscar Grusky and George A. Miller. New York: The Free Press, 1970.

Lopata, Helena Z., "Loneliness: Forms and Components," Social Problems, 17 (1969), 248-62. Reprinted in Robert S. Weiss, ed. Loneliness: The Experience of Emotional and Social Isolation. Cambridge, Mass.: MIT Press, 1973.

_____, Occupation: Housewife. New York: Oxford University Press, 1971.

————, *Widowhood in an American City.* Cambridge, Mass.: Schenkman Publishing Co., General Learning Press, 1973. (a)

————, "The Effect of Schooling on Social Contacts of Urban Women," *American Journal of Sociology,* 79 (1973); 604–19. (b)

————, "Support Systems of Widows," report to the Social Security Administration, 1975. (a)

————, "Couple Companionate Relationships in Marriage and Widowhood," in *Old Family/New Family,* ed. Nona Glazer Malbin. New York: D. Van Nostrand, 1975. (b)

Lowenthal, Marjorie, and C. Haven, "Interaction and Adaptation: Intimacy as a Critical Variable," *American Sociological Review,* 33 (1968), 20–30.

Packard, Vance, *The Status Seekers.* New York: Cardinal Pocket Books, 1961.

————, *The Pyramid Climbers.* Greenwich, Conn.: Fawcett Crest, 1962.

Rosow, Irving, *The Social Integration of the Aged.* New York: The Free Press of Macmillan, 1967.

Weber, Max, *The Protestant Ethic and the Spirit of Capitalism.* London: George Allen & Unwin, 1930.

Weiss, Robert S., *Loneliness: The Experience of Emotion and Social Isolation.* Cambridge, Mass.: The MIT Press, 1973.

Whyte, William H., Jr., *The Organization Man.* New York: Simon & Schuster, 1956.

Znaniecki, Florian, *Social Relations and Social Roles.* San Francisco: Chandler Publishing Co., 1965.

Chapter 10

What Do Women Use Friends For?

Sandra E. Gibbs Candy

As the years go by, most of us accumulate a few friends to whom we feel close and whose company we enjoy. These friends may be different from each other, with distinctive personalities and individual lifestyles. What is it that draws us to *these* particular people and not to others? Is there something special about them that makes us feel close to them? What do they do for us that makes us want to share our moments of joy, of sorrow, or of boredom and that compels us to phone or write them when we are apart? In particular, do older women use friends for different purposes than do younger women?

In order to answer such questions, I contacted women between 14 and 80 who were either high school students, teachers, or retired teachers, and asked them to describe their relationship with their five closest friends—to say what they used these friends for.

Although most previous research shows that adults have only three or four close friends, it is interesting to note that *all* of these women had no problem talking about five close friends and most indicated that they had even more friends than this. Of course high school students and teachers are out of the house much more than the traditional housewives studied before. It is also interesting that these five closest or "best" friends were people they had known for many years, in the case of the older women, and at least two years in

Sandra E. Gibbs Candy is a psychology graduate student at Wayne State University. Her research is developmental changes in friendship throughout life.

the case of the younger. There seems to be some truth to the old adage, "There's no friend like an old friend."

FRIENDS ARE WOMEN AND WOMEN ARE FRIENDS

Over 80 percent of the friends described were female. And the women over 50 had even a greater percentage of female friends (87 percent). Some writers believe that friendship with the opposite sex is considered dangerous because it could lead to extramarital intimacy. Apparently, friendship is primarily a same-sex bond. Even if older women want men friends, however, they are at a disadvantage because of the unequal proportion of surviving men to women. (This is of course assuming that older women do not consider friendship with younger nonrelated males either comfortable or appropriate.) An alternative explanation for the prevalance of female friendships may be because they offer something that friendship with men does not. Not only will two women have more experiences in common and thus understand each other better but women in general find it easier to get closer to others and to disclose more "secrets" than men do (Jourard, 1958). As will be seen later, women feel that intimacy is absolutely necessary in a friendship, though few men feel comfortable discussing their feelings.

RELATIVES

Relatives were not usually considered "best friends" by the women in this study. On the average, only 25 percent of all close friends were relatives. However, if a relative was named as one of the closest friends, it tended to be a female cousin if the respondent was an adolescent, a husband or sister if she was between 20 and 60, and a daughter or sister if she was over 60 years old. It is interesting that many young and middle-aged women do consider their husband their best friend. Some writers feel that this type of "double relationship" results in role confusion. On the other hand, both Greeley (1970) and Lepp (1966) state that friendship and marriage are *not* mutually exclusive. In fact, they say that if marriage is not a friendship it is not a satisfactory human relationship.

In late adulthood, when the frequency of widowhood in-creases, the number and geographic closeness of children may af-fect friendship. Riley and her colleagues (1972) found that when bonds between older people and their adult children are weak or missing, friends and neighbors become more important. Among the women over 60 in the present study, one-third of their friends who were relatives were daughters who lived nearby. But most of their best or closest friends were nonrelatives whom they had known for a long time. What purpose did these friendships serve? The answers of all of the women studied (from 14 to 80) showed three important purposes: intimacy-assistance, status giving, and power and influence.

INTIMACY-ASSISTANCE

Unburdening of secrets seems to work like giving or getting help. Apparently, friends help by giving emotional support, finan-cial support, or comfort as the occasion requires. A friend is some-one who gives all three and from whom one can accept all three. Lowenthal and Haven (1968) report that having a confidante eases major life adjustments at all ages. A confidante can support us, validate our beliefs, and act as a "sounding board" when we need to "let off steam."

The women in this study, of all ages, reported that *all* of their close friends were used for intimacy and help. It appears that to be considered a friend one *must* serve this double function.

STATUS

Friends are also used for "status." Women revealed that they "liked to be seen with their friend" as it "made them feel important" or caused "others to look up to them because they knew this par-ticular person." This is particularly true for teenagers, who may feel that friendship with someone of perceived higher status helps define their own self-worth. High school sophomore Sally Weiss may become friends with football hero Tom Redmond, or with socially popular Sue Hill, in order to increase her own social standing, even though she may not share any interests with Sue or have any deep concern for Tom. The use of friends for status purposes decreases from the teens through the 50s. Such a relationship tends to be superficial, because one is not emotionally involved but puts more emphasis on outward appearance. With increasing age, women tend to develop deeper, more understanding, and more meaningful relationships that are also characterized by more reciprocity.

The retired teachers in this study, however, used their friends more for "status" purposes than any other age group, even the adolescents. How much of this difference is because they are an unusual group of women and how much is true of older women in general, we cannot say. Fifty-eight percent of these older retired women were not married (either never married, divorced, or widowed), and *all* held at least a bachelor's decree. Other studies have found that recognition by others is valued more by nonmarried, educated, and older women than by married, less educated, and younger women (Bickel, 1968). Thus, the older women living today who are nonmarried and educated may have *always*, even as adolescents, placed a high value on gaining approval and recognition from others.

One can also speculate that these retired teachers, who had worked for many years, experienced a negative change in social position. A decrease or loss in social position after retirement could be compensated for by increasing one's evaluation of the "status" characteristics in friends. Since the great majority of these retired women had maintained their friends over many years, they are probably reevaluating their friendship, not selecting new friends to serve this purpose. They may *perceive* their old friends as more important people than they had previously, although in all truth they are no doubt the same individuals they always were. Since retirees spend more time interacting with their friends (Cottrell and Atchley, 1969), they see them as more important, which in turn renews the prestige they themselves lost upon retirement.

POWER

The third major use of friends by women is for the purpose of "power," of having authority or influence over them or, reciprocally, being influenced by them. We can get friends to do things for us, or just have the pleasure of being in command, making us feel important. There is a steady decrease in this use of friends from adolescence through the late 50s, but the older women (60 and over) show a very slight increase. This over-60 increase may reflect the same needs for regaining importance after retirement that I discussed with reference to status.

BEST FRIEND

There seems to be a distinction between a "best friend" and all other friends. As the closeness of a friend decreases (from best to fifth best) she is not used as much for any of the three purposes previously mentioned. Even though women use *all* of their friends for intimacy-assistance, status, and power, they distinguish between a "best friend" and others by demanding more of the same from this one special person. This was true for women of all ages.

It has been suggested that we can tolerate only so much reciprocal intimacy with others. If so, an increase of self- disclosures or secret revelations to one friend must be accompanied by a decrease to other friends (Kaplan, 1974). This is what appears to be happening in these women. Most say they share deep confidences only with a few.

Without any doubt there is something special about a woman's very close friends. Older women use friends for the same purposes as do younger women, but most of them agree that such old friends are impossible to replace. Since most of their close friends are old friends, years of interaction have been invested in them.

REFERENCES

Bickel, H. E., "An Analysis of the Work Values of Women: Implications for Counseling," *Dissertation Abstracts,* 69, No. 6688 (1968).

Cottrell, F., and R. Atchley, *Women in Retirement: A Preliminary Report.* Oxford, Ohio: Scripps Foundation, 1969.

Erikson, E. H., *Childhood and Society.* New York: W. W. Norton and Co., Inc., 1950.

Greeley, A., *The Friendship Game.* New York: Doubleday, 1970.

Jourard, S. M., and P. Lasakow, "Some Factors in Self- Disclosure," *Journal of Abnormal and Social Psychology,* 56 (1958), 91–98.

Kaplan, K. J., "Structure and Process in Interpersonal Distancing," paper presented at symposium on "Some New Approaches for Studying and Measuring Interpersonal Communication," 82nd Annual Meeting of the A.P.A., New Orleans, Louisiana, September 1974.

Lepp, I., *The Ways of Friendship*, trans. Bernard Murchland. New York: Macmillan Co., 1966.

Lowenthal, M. F., and C. Haven, "Interaction and Adaptation: Intimacy as a Critical Variable, in *Middle Age and Aging*, pp. 390-400. ed. B. L. Neugarten. Chicago: University of Chicago Press, 1968.

Riley, M., M. Johnson, and A. Foner, "Friends and Neighbors, in *Aging and Society, a Sociology of Age Stratification*, Vol. 1, 289-313, ed. M. Riley et al. New York: Russell Sage Foundation, 1972.

PART IV

New Worlds

This section deals with new ways to go—in work, education, and recreation. There also have been astonishing breakthroughs and opportunities for older women in community and religious activities, and politics.

Increasing numbers of middle-aged women are returning to the labor force, both in traditional and nontraditional jobs. This influx has been creating new relationships and conditions for women both in the way they see themselves, their families see them, and society sees them. Even retirement does not necessarily close off the meaningful activities of work, as the foster grandparent and similar projects demonstrate. Many middle-aged and older women of today had to take second place in getting an education. Where resources were limited—and they were for many during the Depression— sons took precedence over daughters. Over the past decade, due to the convergence of numerous societal forces, women are streaming back to institutions of higher learning, most for occupational purposes, but some for intellectual stimulation. Once having tasted the experiences of learning and of interaction with other students, hundreds of women are finding "they cannot go home again." As for recreation, women are moving a long way from the sewing circle and the garden club. Tours to exotic far places, sports groups and tournaments from bowling to tennis, and even direct participation in politics, making decisions not only coffee, all provide new paths which today's older women are exploring.

Chapter 11

Women and Leisure

Jon A. Hendricks

"I'm short, fat, and 45." So begins a peppery initiate to a consciousness-raising group of middle-aged women gathered for the
first time to help one another take measure of what they might do
with their lives over the coming years (Jacoby, 1973). It is no easy
task thinking two decades into the future, and for this rap session in
East Flatbush or the countless others meeting around the country
the hurdles frequently appear insurmountable. For the first time in
history large numbers of women must grapple with redefinition of
their identities, relationships, and goals in midlife. Traditionally
most women have not been confronted by such a problem.
Childrearing stretched out over much of their adult lives and it was
not at all out of the ordinary for one or the other marital partner to
have died before the last child left home. However, with the com-
pression of the family life cycle, a growing number of women find
themselves near the end of what they have been raised to believe is
their life's work, though they themselves are just entering middle
age. To attain anything approaching an adequate grasp of the adjustments facing women in their middle years, it is necessary to
understand the role leisure and free-time activities play in their

Jon A. Hendricks, Ph.D., is on the faculty of the Department of Sociology at the
University of Kentucky. His interests are wide—including the study of time, leisure, and
various other aspects of aging.

lives. Yet, as is often the case, precious little is known in advance about what middle age will be like or what other women experience. Unfortunately, even the fanfare accompanying the first International Women's Year in 1975 did not include any appreciable attention to middle-aged or older women. At the inaugural conference in Mexico City and at other sessions held throughout the year, the life and leisure of older women was largely neglected (*Ageing International*, 1975).

Even a brief review of women's leisure activities is sufficient to indicate that middle age does not carry with it changes nearly as drastic as popular stereotypes might have us believe. Although the focus and nature of certain forms of leisure may shift, the available evidence does not suggest a widespread adoption of new activities. Continuity is more often the order of the day. The present generation of women in midlife represents what might be termed an advance guard. Their leisure can be distinguished from what their mothers enjoyed, and probably portends what women tomorrow and the day after may experience. There is greater involvement in existing free-time pursuits often accompanied by a return to those interests which have been neglected for a number of years.

WHAT IS A WOMAN TO DO?

Today many women in midlife return to the labor market or enter it for the first time. While the facts about this are fairly well-known, comparatively little information is available regarding women's use of discretionary (leisure) time. For twenty years or more their so-called leisure has been structured by family relationships or by those resources available to them within the context of their homemaker roles. In middle age, for perhaps the first time, a woman has the opportunity to seek out her own recreational activities. Some women react to this much like workers who are suddenly displaced into the ranks of the unemployed. Instead of expanding their leisure pursuits into the time previously occupied by work or work-related activities, they may actually contract their "leisure" time. Of course this is not true of all women. For some, release from the tyranny of either the clock or domestic chores makes possible all manner of meaningful activities. A woman who does not work for pay outside the home enjoys considerable fluidity in her time budget. She can establish a rhythm of her own choosing, which her sisters who hold outside jobs cannot. Having acknowledged these basic conditions, the most obvious question is how middle-aged women utilize whatever discretionary time they have.

Leisure is one of those paradoxical areas of life—one person's leisure may represent another's unadulterated drudgery. An illustration particularly applicable to women has to do with the whole realm of consumption. Within each family a division of labor exists; this may be either very formal, with specific duties to be performed by the parties involved, or quite informal, with the family's roles assigned on an *ad hoc* or task-by-task basis. In many cases the functional division of family responsibilities extends to leisure, resulting in such patterns as the man deciding where the family might go for a picnic, and the woman determining what they are to eat. Likewise, men wash the car or tend the yard and women shop for and select the consumer goods the family intends to purchase. A large portion of a woman's free time is really a kind of consumption time in which she makes the rounds of stores, evaluating the best buys. Indeed it may well be that consumption, either material or symbolic, is an essential ingredient of much of the leisure characteristic of advanced industrial societies (Hendricks, 1974). A thoughtful scrutiny of the advertising pitches for major lines of consumer goods may easily leave one feeling that women do little else with their discretionary time than attend to the family's purchases (de Grazia, 1964). Regardless of the advertising agencies' druthers, this is not entirely accurate. In point of fact, shopping only consumes an average of over an hour daily in the lives of both housewives and working women in the United States (Szalai et al., 1972).

Obviously, whether or not a woman works outside the home has a major impact on the nature of her leisure. In a study of time budgets in twelve countries, Szalai and his colleagues (1972) found, not surprisingly, that housewives without outside jobs had the greatest amount of time remaining after meeting their obligations. They in turn were followed by employed men, while employed married women had the least amount of uncommitted time of all three groups. This pattern varies according to the day of the week. Although the full-time housewife has more "free time" during the week, she has less on Sundays. Parenthetically, we might note that while the advent of "flexitime" would allow male employees to rearrange their hours of work to enhance their leisure, the advantages they gain may well be at the expense of wives who will have to accommodate their personal schedules to those of other family members. Labor-saving gadgets, incidentally, do not yeild any particular opportunities for increased leisure. Instead, the effect of such devices is to relieve housewives of tedious or physically taxing

Table 1

Percentage of Free Time Allocated to Various
Leisure Activities in Twelve Countries*

	Employed Men	Employed Women	Housewives
Education	6	4	1
Religion	1	2	2
Organizations	2	2	1
—Study Participation	9	8	4
Radio	4	3	3
TV (home)	23	23	24
TV (away)	1	1	1
Newspapers	8	4	4
Magazines	1	2	2
Books	4	5	4
Movies	2	3	1
—Mass Media	43	41	39
Socializing (home)	5	6	6
Socializing (away)	9	9	9
Conversation	6	6	7
Sports	1	1	—
Outdoor Activities	7	5	6
Entertainment	2	2	1
Cultural Involvements	—	1	—
Resting	8	9	11
Other Leisure	3	8	13
Leisure Traveling	7	7	5
—Other Leisure	48	54	58
	100%	100%	100%
Average free time daily	4½ hrs.	3½ hrs.	4½ hrs.

Source: J. P. Robinson, P. E. Converse, and A. Szalai, "Everyday Life in Twelve Countries," in A. Szalai *et al.*, *The Use of Time.* The Hague: Mouton and Co., 1972, p. 132. Reprinted by permission.

*Rounding may affect totals.

chores, only to foster a turning of attention to other household tasks (Szalai et al., 1972).

Undoubtedly there are noteworthy differences in the leisure enterprises of people in the twelve countries as a consequence of ethnic and cultural backgrounds. Nevertheless, there does emerge a marked similarity in the broad use of free time. The patterning of reported leisure activities is presented in Table 1. These figures should be interpreted cautiously, since methodological considerations play a role beyond the scope of our discussion here. For example, conversations represent only 6 or 7 percent of the leisure time for all three groups. Yet people clearly spend much more time than that talking with friends in the process of carrying out some other activity. An analysis of secondary activities, those seen as accompanying or concurrent with but not necessarily motivating forces, reveals that this is indeed the case. Approximately three hours are spent daily in various forms of conversation. The significant point to bear in mind in looking over the table is that many forms of leisure occur simultaneously. It is quite likely that these figures underestimate the extent and importance of certain forms of leisure.

LEISURE IN THE MIDDLE YEARS AND BEYOND

Contrary to popular opinion, women in their middle years do not experience an overabundance of free time. In fact, the number of women who report a feeling of being shortchanged in terms of leisure reaches a peak in the ages between 46 and 55. Why this should be true is a question open to any number of answers, all of which are certainly plausible. It has become clear that the majority of women do not attribute to middle age the emptiness that is often assumed (Pfeiffer and Davis, 1974). Only a few are left hanging by the departure of their children. What tends to happen is a change in the locale and focus of their leisure activities. Previously, much of the lifestyle of a married woman was shaped and molded by her roles of wife and mother. What free time she did enjoy was geared to the schedules of her husband or children. Thus a large portion of her leisure did not necessitate a great deal of advance planning of major time expenditures in single blocks. Women whose children are already launched turn more to community-based leisure and less to home-based leisure. At the same time, they are more likely to develop "self-enriching" forms of leisure, including various forms of adult education, cultural involvements, and organizational activity not specifically oriented to their status as wives or mothers. Even when the range of organizational memberships is not altered over the years, the extent of involvement becomes greater among older women (Angrist, 1967; Searls, 1966).

One of the age-related changes associated with leisure among women is a tendency to increase the time devoted to socializing activities. Participation in such groups as bridge clubs, women's clubs, and so on gradually expands throughout middle age. The popular caricature of "soap operas" as an important aspect of the daily routine of many women who do not work outside the home may have some validity. Notwithstanding common avowals of their lack of discretionary time, women do spend more time watching television. Until middle age, men watch more than women, but during their late 40s and 50s the amount of time women spend in front of the TV surpasses that of their male counterparts (Pfeiffer and Davis, 1974). Hobbies also reemerge as an area in which women extend their involvements during midlife. Interestingly enough, the importance of shopping as a form of leisure does not decrease with middle age as might be expected with a lessening of family responsibilities. Presumably for some women the shopping trip serves as a kind of outing, to be shared with friends or as an opportunity to observe contemporary lifestyles by wandering through stores without feeling bound to purchase much of anything. Although these trips may take place at any time, they tend to become concentrated on weekdays during the later morning or early afternoon, sometimes entailing luncheon meetings with other women. For those who have always been so inclined, volunteer work becomes more predominant, as do club activities, neither of which especially require or encourage male companionship. These too are generally confined to weekdays, with the weekend remaining reserved for family or home-centered activities.

Perhaps the most sweeping generalization possible is that few women manifest anything that might be considered a radical change in middle life, either in terms of family duties or leisure. It cannot be stressed too strongly, also, that social, economic, racial, and ethnic differences are important. Generally speaking, women confront a redistribution of the competing demands of family, work, and leisure two decades in advance of a comparable adjustment by men. Since they also live longer, what are nominally called the retirement years are twice as long for women. Without adequate preparation, it does not necessarily follow that these are leisure years. Without integrating leisure activities into the overall scheme and patterning of their life, women will fail to reap the fruits of their labors.

REFERENCES

Ageing International, "Older Women Neglected in International Women's Year?", 2, No.4 (1975), 2-3.

Angrist, Shirley S., "Role Constellation as a Variable in Women's Leisure Activities," *Social Forces,* 45 (1967), 423-31.

de Grazia, Sebastian, *Of Time, Work and Leisure.* Garden City, N.Y.: Anchor Books, 1964.

Dumazedier, Joffre, *Toward a Society of Leisure,* p. 98. New York: The Free Press, 1967.

Havighurst, R. J., and K. Feigenbaum, "Leisure and Lifestyle," *American Journal of Sociology,* 64 (1959), 396-404.

Hendricks, Jon, "Emergence and Maintenance of Self-Concept Through Leisure: The Ozymandian Process," a paper presented to World Congress of Sociology, Toronto, Canada, 1974.

Jacoby, Susan, "What Do I Do for the Next 20 Years?", The *New York Times Magazine,* June 17, 1973.

Pfeiffer, Eric, and Glenn C. Davis, "The Use of Leisure in Middle Life," in *Normal Aging II,* ed. E. Palmore, pp. 232-43. Durham, N.C.: Duke University Press, 1974.

Searls, Laura G. "Leisure Role Emphasis of College Graduate Homemakers," *Journal of Marriage and the Family,* 28, No. 1 (February 1966), 77-82.

Sussman, Marvin B., "Activity Patterns of Post-Parental Couples and their Relationship to Family Continuity," *Marriage and Family Living,* 17 (November 1955), 338-41.

Szalai, Alexander, et al., *The Use of Time: Daily Activities of Urban and Suburban Populations in Twelve Countries.* The Hague: Mouton and Co., 1972.

Thompson, Wayne F., and Gordon F. Strieb, "Meaningful Activity in a Family Context," in *Aging and Leisure,* ed. R. W. Kleemeier, pp. 177-211. New York: Oxford University Press, 1961.

Chapter 12

Older Women and Jobs

Robert C. Atchley / Sherry L. Corbett

Not only has little attention been paid to how a job fits into the life of an older woman, but what has received even less attention is how retirement affects her. More and more older women are in the labor force and more are holding jobs that have traditionally, been thought of as "men's work" (Waldman, 1972). Yet research in this area is so sparse that much of what we have to say here is speculative.

One of the most common statements about women and jobs is that women work for different reasons than men do, that they get a different meaning from working, or that jobs have a different place in their value system. Yet when we consider the wide diversity among jobs, such a statement seems simplistic. Jobs vary from sanitation worker to Supreme Court Justice. Some provide all kinds of rewards and gratifications and others are at best a chore. Some do not pay enough to support one person and some provide more than ample support for dozens. It is not surprising, therefore, as

Robert C. Atchley, Ph.D., is Professor of Sociology and Director of the Scripps Foundation at Miami University, Oxford, Ohio. He is the author of *The Social Forces in Later Life*, *The Sociology of Retirement*, *Understanding American Society*, and *The Sociology of Aging* (with Mildred Seltzer), as well as numerous articles. Two of his main interests are migration and retirement. Sherry L. Corbett, Ph.D., is Assistant Professor of Sociology and Anthropology in the Department of Sociology at Miami University, Oxford, Ohio. Her major areas of interest are in social deviance and gerontology.

Friedmann and Havighurst (1954) found, that jobs have widely different meanings.

One way to rate the value of a job is to determine whether it provides opportunity for achievement. It is often assumed that women do not usually find achievement important. However, even though research shows that women do not follow the same achievement patterns as men, that jobs may have different meanings for them, they are just as likely as men to feel that being good at a job is an important life goal (Atchley, 1976).

One factor that is common to all jobs, regardless of their other characteristics, is that they offer socially visible rewards—like receiving a pay check, ways of knowing that you have done well. Being a good mother or a good housewife is hard work but it cannot do this. Rewards for good work in these non-job areas are, on the one hand, private and, on the other hand, not guaranteed. Such rewards are also not as impressive as those provided by jobs because they are bestowed by people (family members) whom one might suspect of being somewhat biased in their evaluations. In contrast, the rewards associated with jobs are more widely accepted in society. They can be compared with the rewards other people get. Pay and promotion provide standards by which people can measure their achievement against that of others. And these standards are very important to women. Thus, even though a job as such may not be particularly rewarding, women can get great satisfaction just from having one.

Many women today enter the job market in their 40s or 50s, often after having "gone back to school." While this can be a difficult transition, it can also have many good points. For one thing, many people, both men and women, find a new job revitalizing and leading to growth. It involves not only using new skills but also meeting new people, developing new routines, modifying old relationships, and a host of other subtle changes that can be exciting and challenging. Whether a job change is seen as challenging or as aggravating depends partly on how hard it is for a person to adapt to change in general. However, most people cope well with change, particularly if they initiate it themselves. And this is true of most women who enter the labor force in midlife (Busse and Pfeiffer, 1969).

A job can mean freedom, independence, and economic self-sufficiency for an older woman. It can justify unloading tedious household chores on other members of the household. And it can free her from an artificial suburban world that is peopled only by women and children and provide contacts with a broader social atmosphere and a greater diversity of lifestyles and people.

There is a negative side, though. Entry into the labor force may simply add to a woman's burden. Although she may not have as much of the actual work around the house as before, she usually still has complete *responsibility* for running the household, and, in fact, may just be adding on another kind of work without getting free of her housework. Because working-class women are less likely to be able to delegate the household chores when they add on an outside job than are middle-class women, they are more likely to end up with more negative attitudes about working.

Let us consider the issue of how jobs fit into the overall context of older women's lives. In American society it is possible for men to become almost completely absorbed by their jobs. This is more difficult for women. In part, this difference comes from our basic social norms. A woman is not supposed to make her job that important. In fact, those women who are highly committed to being good at a job are likely to be punished in one way or another. This is particularly true for any woman who leaves her husband and children in order to pursue a career on a full-time basis. The norms of our society do not so much discourage women from developing commitments to jobs as they discourage the development of such commitment *to the exclusion of other things*. And this (rather than different kinds of commitment to jobs) may be what differentiates women's orientation toward jobs from men's orientation.

In general, husbands and families are likely to exert pressure on women to play down their jobs as life goals. That this pressure is not altogether effective is reflected by data showing that 60 percent of working women rank being considered good at their work among the three most important goals in their life (Atchley, 1976). The effects of the "empty nest" and of widowhood also increase the centrality of jobs in the lives of older women. Many women cope with these changes by increasing their commitment to their job.

Women are less likely than men to have "normal" career patterns. While men usually follow a continuous career line, women often have sporadic employment experiences owing to disruptions caused by marriage and childrearing. For instance, a male university graduate in petroleum engineering may be recruited by a major oil company. He is likely to be sent to the field as an apprentice, and after a training period brought into the company office. Then, if he is sufficiently competent and committed to his job, he will eventually fill a slot in junior management. There is programmed continuity in his movement within the corporate structure.

In contrast, a female high school graduate, not being given the financial resources to go to college like her brother, may take a job in a factory. She will marry a man who makes enough money to support her and a new family. Her work experience will be interrupted when she becomes a housewife. Later, when she sends her last child off to grade school, she may consider reentry into the work force. At this point, options are limited by prejudices against older workers, inexperienced workers, and female workers. If she is able to use her by now rusty high school typing and shorthand skills, she manages to find a job as an office clerk, where any hopes for advancement are limited, not only by systematic discrimination but also by educational and experiential deficits. Because of discrimination against women in hiring practices, income differentials, and differential prospects for advancement, women tend to end up in "dead-end" jobs much more frequently than men do. For example, male teachers in secondary schools may eventually move into administrative positions; their female counterparts remain classroom teachers.

Because of their late entry into the labor force, female "late bloomers" may not have enough time to advance along the customary career milestones, and thus are more likely to feel extreme goal frustration. They will feel particularly bad at having to leave their job because of compulsory retirement.

Just as work orientation is tied to the quality of a job, so is adjustment to retirement. The extent of disruption created by retirement depends on how much it changes a person's life and the capacity of that person to deal with change in a flexible manner. In turn, the amount of change is related to the hierarchy of personal goals. The more important a job is to a person, or the higher it is in that person's hierarchy of goals, the more disrupting retirement would be. If a woman can consolidate her remaining roles after retirement, then she may have a simple and painless transition. Retirement is typically seen as a man's life crisis. He is more often seen as a "breadwinner" and his job as providing both income and meaning to life. Since the primary traditional female roles are those of wife, housekeeper, and mother, the woman's work outside the home has been considered less significant. If this is true, she should be able to focus on her wife-related roles after retirement.

There are several flaws in this line of reasoning. First, as indicated previously, a job may be just as important for a woman as for a man. She is just as likely to be highly committed to it. Retirement could therefore result in "withdrawal symptoms" for women as well as men.

Second, the assumption that women can easily refocus to "in-home" roles ignores the fact that it was partly because of the loss of such roles in middle age that they initially became involved in jobs. Most women at retirement have no children living at home and 30 percent are widows (Atchley, 1975). It is therefore no surprise that women tend to take longer than men to adjust to retirement (Atchley, 1976).

Third, because they have gotten a late career start, their retirement is likely to come before their job goals are achieved.

The analysis in this chapter is based on studies of older women today. Upcoming generations of women may not have the same job history as those now retiring. Ironically, if women's relations to their jobs grow more like those of men, retirement could become an easier transition for them than it is now.

REFERENCES

Atchley, R. C., "Adjustment to Loss of Job at Retirement," *International Journal of Aging and Human Development,* 6 (1975), 17–28.

_____, "Selected Psychological and Social Differences Among Men and Women in Later Life," *Journal of Gerontology,* 31 (1976), 204–11.

Busse, E. W., and E. Pfeiffer, eds., *Behavior and Adaptation in Later Life.* Boston: Little, Brown and Co., 1969.

Friedmann, E., and R. Havighurst, *The Meaning of Work and Retirement.* Chicago: University of Chicago Press, 1954.

Streib, G. F., and C. J. Schneider, *Retirement in American Society.* Ithaca, N. Y.: Cornell University Press, 1971.

Waldman, E., "Changes in the Labor Force Activity of Women," in *Woman in a Man-Made World,* ed. Nona Glazer-Malbin and Helen Waehrer. Chicago: Rand McNally and Co., 1972.

Chapter 13

Fostergrandparenting:
A Unique Child-Care Service *

Rosalyn Saltz

Both working and nonworking women face critical alterations in their life circumstances as they age. While 50 percent of all American women between the ages of 40 and 59 are in the labor force, only 9 percent are still working after age 60 (U. S. Census, 1973). Many of these older women have marginal incomes. Of those who are not living with relatives, 45 percent have an income below the poverty level, and in minority groups this figure rises to about 65 percent. The older woman, then, often confronts a combination of bitter problems that represent major barriers to her life satisfaction: loss of loved ones, loss of her primary role identity, fading self-esteem, increasing social isolation, and financial distress.

Can society find practical, effective ways to alleviate these problems and thus improve the quality of life? Several successful programs both in and out of government over the past decade suggest that this is possible. These programs all involve the utilization of older persons in various social service roles. By offering them op-

Rosalyn Saltz, Ph.D., is an associate professor in the Department of Education, University of Michigan, Dearborn. Her primary interest in child care has involved her in establishing and evaluating fostergrandparent programs in this country and in Italy.

*The writer wishes to express her gratitude to Mr. John Keller, Deputy Director, U.S. Older Americans Program, and Miss Rita Katzman, Director of the Wayne County, Michigan Fostergrandparent Program, Catholic Social Services of Wayne County, for providing her with current (1976) statistics on the U.S. and Detroit area Fostergrandparent Programs.

portunities to be of useful service to others (in some cases in exchange for small stipends), to take on new, positive social identities, and to form new social attachments, such programs have hoped to meet the major unmet life-satisfaction needs of many older men and women.

The U. S. Fostergrandparent Program, currently sponsored by the federal agency, ACTION, was a pioneer in this area, and is probably the largest and most widely known of the programs that aim to assist older persons by offering them an opportunity to serve others. The basic goal of all such programs is clearly expressed in a Fostergrandparent Program announcement offering "a retirement *to* something instead of a retirement *from* something" (U.S. ACTION, 1975). This particular program aims to benefit mutually both older persons and children by creating a new child-care service role, "fostergrandparenting." a role that seems particularly suited to the needs and talents of many older women.

Fostergrandparents are low-income individuals over the age of 60 who are part-time caregivers in group settings for children. Under the direction of professional staff, they generally serve four hours daily, five days a week, and are assigned to settings such as residential institutions for dependent and neglected, mentally retarded, emotionally disturbed, or physically handicapped children, as well as to some correctional facilities, pediatric wards of hospitals, and day-care centers and classrooms. Each fostergrandparent receives a stipend, transportation allowance, accident insurance, free lunch, and an annual physical examination. No special educational qualifications are required, but fostergrandparents must complete a forty-hour preservice training program and are involved in regular group and individual in-service training sessions. As of the end of 1975, there were 13,600 fostergrandparents serving in 156 projects throughout the fifty states, the District of Columbia, and Puerto Rico. Four out of five were women. They ranged in age from 60 to 106. (In 1975, 35 percent of fostergrandparents were between the ages of 65 and 70, 44 percent were over 70 years of age, and 18 percent were over 75 years of age.)

A fostergrandparent is a member of a child-care team whose special function is to form a quasi-familial, personal relationship with specific children within group settings by giving them special attention and affection. Each fostergrandparent is assigned to only two children. Depending on the nature of the setting and the age and needs of each child, a fostergrandparent might hold and comfort or rock a young child, work with an older child on academic skills or therapeutic regimes, play games, admire a new achievement or production, read a story, be a confidante, or simply sit by while a preschooler is playing with peers, always available to tie a shoelace, praise, gently scold, or give a hug as circumstances require. The intense bond that is fostered and, in fact, tends to develop quickly between a fostergrandparent and child is obvious when the older person proudly tells visitors of the special virtues, progress, and accomplishments of "*My* Billy!" or "*My* Mary" or conversely, when Billy or Mary wait eagerly at the door for "*My* grandma" or throw arms around "grandma" at her arrival.

At this writing, the ten-year old U.S. Fostergrandparent Program appears to be achieving its goal of improving life adjustment and satisfaction for aging persons—i.e., of offering older persons the opportunity for "a retirement *to*" something worthwhile. As one long-term foster grandmother said to this interviewer, "I *worked* all my life. *This* is pleasure." Another reported, "It [the Fostergrandparent Program] has made a new life for me. Each day is a new adventure. It's the most wonderful experience I ever had," and a third maintained that the fostergrandparent experience "proves retired senior citizens don't have to be put on the shelf!"

Several objective studies support informal impressions of the program's success. An intensive, long-term study focusing on one of the first Fostergrandparent Programs in the United States, operated by Catholic Social Services of Wayne County and located in a children's home in the Detroit area, found marked positive effects for both the older persons and the young institutionalized children who participated in the program (Saltz, 1971, 1973). Clear developmental benefits were found for the children. For the older persons, fostergrandparenting was associated with greatly increased self-esteem, renewed feelings of health and vigor, satisfying social relationships, a gratifying sense of activity and a new sense of purpose in day-to-day life, and increased satisfaction with financial circumstances.

A recent, broadly based national study supports the Detroit-area findings. This latter study, which surveyed a large (20 percent) representative sample of all Fostergrandparent Programs throughout the United States, again found very beneficial effects for both children and fostergrandparents (Booz, Allen, 1972). Almost 90 percent of the fostergrandparents in the national sample reported generally increased feelings of life satisfaction, less financial worry, increased feelings of usefulness, self-respect, and independence, decreased feelings of social isolation, and increased feelings of being loved. Seventy-five percent felt that the fostergrandparenting experience was one of the most important events in their life during the past five years.

The program's success is also indicated by the rather remarkable service longevity record of fostergrandparents. Only 10 percent of the total national group of 13,600 fostergrandparents terminated their services in the last half of 1975. After ten years, almost one-half of the original Detroit-area study sample was still serving as fostergrandparents.

In any evaluation study, responses to interview questions must be categorized, coded, and summarized to give quantifiable results for purposes of analysis and reporting (e.g., in this case in terms of how responses might relate to possible effects on life-satisfaction dimensions such as health, opportunity for activity, etc.). However, the true flavor and meaning of the impact of an experience such as fostergrandparenting on the lives of the older persons in the program cannot be understood from such abstracted, quantified summaries alone. Can one fully quantify the comment of one older woman in the Fostergrandparent Program (reported by U.S. ACTION, 1975), who said, "when I used to wake up in an empty house, I felt I was the only person in the world who was alone. . . . This program turned me around, gave me something to live for!"

In the Detroit-area study, one of the questions asked of fostergrandparents who had completed at least two years of service was, "What benefits, if any, do you think the fostergrandparents got from their work?" The following examples of some responses to this question, along with some of the major areas of benefit these responses illustrate, may give further insight into the concrete meaning of the fostergrandparent experience from the point of view of the older persons themselves:

1. *Improved self-esteem* (pride in being useful, needed). "I am happier than in many years, to feel, at my age, that I am able to do something to help others." "I hope to say, in later years, I helped that boy." "I'm proud of that check. I earned it. It's not welfare. We work for it and see the results of our work in some youngster." "I think it's a wonderful feeling that you're still wanted and still needed."

2. *Purpose to life.* "It [the fostergrandparent experience] gives me something to wake up for, to look forward to the next day." "I am an entirely different person in the two years that I'm here. I feel that I have a goal ahead of me and it's something to look forward to every day."

3. *Social satisfactions.* "If I needed a friend, I know I could call on any one of them." "The group [fostergrandparents] is one big family. "It [the Fostergrandparent Program] makes for warm feelings between people and races."

4. *Subjective feelings of greater health and vigor.* "The program improved my health and my crabby disposition!" "Gave us energy. Otherwise we'd sit and nurse our arthritis." "This work advanced me ten years physically!" "I am able! I am fit! Makes you walk straight!" "My family is amazed at my health!" "I feel better. I have no time for pains." "I know it's done much for all of us health-wise, even the grooming, all of us are better. You can see each day you feel better." "Their [fostergrandparents] health is much better than it would be if they were sitting around without anything to do or anyone to love!"

5. *Financial boost to marginal incomes.* "The extra money means I can keep my home." "I can keep a few pennies. I couldn't before." "Several of them brag, including myself, to the fact that now with what I've got coming in, I am capable of taking care of myself — I don't have to depend on anyone!" "It has really meant a roof over my head. I was able to have my roof fixed!"

Follow-up studies, including a seven-year follow-up of the original Detroit-area fostergrandparent group (Troll, Saltz, Dunin-Markiewicz, 1976) also suggest that many of the benefits, particularly those related to increased self- esteem, persist even after termination from the Fostergrandparent Program.

"I'm proud I was able to do it at *my* age," one former fostergrandmother said. Another, who was forced to leave because of poor health, reflected bittersweet feelings when she recalled: "I miss the place. But it gave me something to think about and never forget. It stays with me. I'll always say, I helped that child. When she came in it was pitiful . . . but when she left, she had come out like a withered plant when you set it in water." She, like most of the others in the terminated group, would agree with the former fostergrandmother who said, "Even now I feel a lot better than before. I feel like I did something good."

What elements of the Fostergrandparent Program have led to

such positive results? As was indicated by the Detroit and national studies, this program clearly offers older persons the much-needed basic benefits discussed earlier: financial aid, a useful role alternative, and an opportunity to enhance self-esteem, engage in regular activity, and develop new social relationships. In addition to these general features, however, the writer believes that fostergrandparenting is an especially suitable and gratifying occupation for many older women because it offers certain unique aspects as compared to other service roles. The formation of very personalized emotional bonds, and the mutuality of emotional need between fostergrandparents and children, may be responsible for much of the program's success in achieving such dramatic benefits for both the older persons and the children involved. When one fostergrandparent reported, "I love him and he loves me. We help each other," she was perhaps summarizing the basic reason for the effectiveness of the fostergrandparent role. For the fostergrandparents, the child's open need of their love and attention is especially gratifying. "I love you, Grandma" is a common, intensely soothing refrain and is balm to wounded egos.

The *mutual* nature of the psychological benefits to the children and the fostergrandparents was gratefully and clearly expressed throughout the research interviews with the fostergrandparent group in the Detroit area study. One fostergrandmother, for example, commented, "I hope and pray I've given one-half as much as I've received." For the children, the worth of the loving service of the fostergrandparents is illustrated in a letter written to a fostergrandparent from a girl in a correctional institution, which read as follows: "When I needed help you were there to listen. I'm going to miss you very much when I leave here. I have tried to be good and I must admit I have done a lot better. I love you like my real grandmother."

Perhaps older women have special motivation and qualifications for serving such a quasi-family function for children despite their knowledge of its temporary nature. Younger caregivers may fear to become too involved if they know a nurturant relationship is to be only temporary. For the older individual, not only is the need for new attachments great, but it seems that if there is satisfaction with the present, there is less tendency to emphasize future possible gratifications or disappointments. Perhaps the present is seen as more important than the future with respect to achieving close, loving relationships because many seem to adhere to the philosophy that, as far as life gratifications are concerned, "The future is *now*." One very low-income widowed woman who had served as a fostergrandparent for several years responded to the research question "What would you need to have the best possible life?" with the answer, "We are living a very good life now. What more is there to get?" Surprisingly, the spirit of this response was quite common among the group of long-term fostergrandparents.

The experience of the Fostergrandparent Program suggests that the present total of just under 14,000 fostergrandparents throughout the United States is very small compared to the number of older persons who could give similar service and to the need on both sides. It would seem that the possibility of rewarding occupations for older women and the potential resource they represent for the field of child services has been barely tapped.

REFERENCES

Booz, Allen, Administration Service, Inc. Cost benefit study of the Fostergrandparent Program. Final Report, Contract SRS-71-41, ACTION, June 1972.

Saltz, R., "Aging Persons as Child-Care Workers in a Fostergrandparent Program: Psychosocial Effects and Work Performance," *Aging and Human Development*, 3 (1971), 314–40.

Saltz, R., "Effects of Part-Time Mothering on IQ and SQ of Young Institutionalized Children," *Child Development*, 44 (1973), 166–70.

Troll, L., R. Saltz, and A. Dunin-Markiewicz, "A Seven-Year Follow-Up of a Group of Fostergrandparents," *Journal of Gerontology*, 31, No. 5 (1976), 583–85.

U.S. ACTION Pamphlet 4500. 7, Washington, D.C., June 1975.

U.S. Bureau of the Census, *Current Population Reports*, Series P-23, No. 43. Some demographic aspects of aging in the United States, Washington, D.C., 1973.

Chapter 14

Lifelong Learning[1]

Nancy K. Schlossberg

I'm a stewardess and back at school because of a nagging feeling that there's more to life than *Coffee, Tea, or Me.*

I'm registered for courses as a way to help me figure out how to be creative in my coming retirement.

I'm here against my husband's and parents' wishes but I'm determined to prepare myself for a career.

I'll keep being passed over for executive positions unless I get more education.

I need something to do now that the children are in school.

These comments, made at a special orientation session for adult women at the University of Maryland, reflect some of the reasons why women of all ages are returning to our college campuses. The social and economic facts of life make it clear that opportunities for lifelong learning are essential to the full development of the individual—female or male—in our society.

To review briefly some familiar but important facts:

Nancy K. Schlossberg, Ph.D., is Professor of Counseling and Guidance at the University of Maryland. She is prominent in the field of counseling adults and continuing education for women. She is co-author, with Lillian Troll, of the book *Perspectives on Counseling Adults* and has written widely on these subjects.

[1]Adapted from testimony delivered to Senate Committee on Education, subcommittee on Labor and Public Welfare, Dec. 18, 1975.

1. The average life expectancy of women has increased in recent years to age 74. At the same time, more women are either remaining single or getting divorced (Lipman-Blumen, 1975).[2] Thus, more women must support themselves, often as heads of households, for longer periods of time, and they need education.

2. Even the woman who follows the traditional route of marriage and childbearing can find herself passing through a "midlife crisis." She has been brought up to believe that only through *vicarious* achievement — that is, through the success of others to whom she is attached — can a woman fulfill herself; she must define her identity through the activities and accomplishments of the dominant people around her: at first her father; then her husband; later her children. But the events of middle life — possible divorce or widowhood, the children's leaving home — throw her back on her own resources, resources that often have been inadequately developed.

3. According to a 1974 survey by the U.S. Department of Labor, "nearly two-thirds of working women are single, divorced, widowed, separated, or have husbands who make less than $7,000 per year" (*Congressional Record,* November 3, 1975). It is obvious, then, that most women work for the same reasons that men work: to support themselves or their families. Yet most remain trapped in low-status, low-paying jobs, such as clerical work. The 15 percent of the female labor force that is employed in the professions tend to cluster in "feminine" fields such as teaching, nursing, library science, and social work. Increasing proportions of female college students aspire to "masculine" fields such as medicine, law, and engineering, but they have not yet reached the labor force. As of 1970, fewer than 10 percent of physicians, about 4.9 percent of lawyers and judges, and 1.5 percent of engineers were women. Moreover, few women hold top administrative positions either in academic areas or in business.

4. Occupational status is highly dependent on educational attainment. Yet women are still progressively filtered out at every level of the educational system. Though more likely to graduate from high school than are men, they are less likely to enroll in college (Carnegie Commission of Higher Education, 1973, p. 35). A smaller proportion of women than of men college graduates take advanced training

[2]Figures, statistics, and interpretations in this section are derived primarily from the work of Jean Lipman-Blumen, Director, Women's Research Program, National Institute of Education, Washington, D.C.

(American Council on Education, 1974, pp. 23-24). Further, women graduate students are more likely than are their male counterparts either to drop out of graduate school or to concentrate in fields in which a master's rather than a doctorate is the required degree.

If women are to improve their lives and enhance their position in the world of work, they must have opportunities for further education. The concept of lifelong learning — of the adult returning to school periodically throughout her life cycle — holds much promise for the future. But the widespread recognition that lifelong learning is both a right and a necessity for the adult woman is only a first step. To make this concept a reality, we must first become aware of, and then do something to reduce or eliminate, the barriers that confront the mature woman who returns to school. Two such barriers will be discussed here: (1) age bias, and (2) limited support services.

BARRIER 1: AGE BIAS

The first barrier, age bias, occurs in every area of academic life; the admissions office, the classroom, the counseling center. It adversely affects the adult man as well as the adult woman, but its consequences are probably more severely detrimental to women since they are more likely to have been discriminated against earlier in their lives. Age bias is reflected both in institutional policies and in the attitudes of faculty, counselors, administrators, and other students.

First a look at institutional barriers. My own experience has brought me into contact with many forms of age discrimination in education: a 37-year-old woman called for my help in getting into dental school; a brilliant woman of 40, eager to move into the federal government, asked me for assistance in changing the age restriction that barred her application as a White House Fellow; a leader in education told me that she was discouraged from applying for entrance to a doctoral program because of her age.

These examples all reflect overt age discrimination. But such bias is often more subtle, as when graduate and professional schools claim nondiscrimination policies which nonetheless impose undue hardships on older women and thus seriously restrict their participation. Take the case of a bright Barnard College graduate who wanted to become a lawyer. She was married and had two small children. With the emotional and financial support of her husband, she entered law school. Her option was either full-time attendance during the day or part-time attendance four nights a week. She opted for full-time study. After two-and-a-half months, as she wrote, "It sounds nice on paper but in real life going to law school full-time is destroying this family and so I quit. If I could have gone part-time during the day, I would have loved it." She is now in an elementary education program.

Many factors that may hinder the older woman in returning to education were recognized by the Carnegie Commission, which made the following recommendation in their 1973 report *Opportunities for Women in Higher Education:*

> Policies that prevent part-time study or that discriminate against admission of adults desirous of continuing their education should be liberalized to permit enrollment of qualified mature men and women whose education has been interrupted because of family responsibilities or for other reasons.

The second type of age bias is perhaps even more difficult to correct, since it involves attitudes and stems from culturally based, deeply embedded "expectations regarding age-appropriate behavior. . . . There exists what might be called a prescriptive timetable for ordering life events: a time in the life span when men and women are expected to marry, go to school, change careers" (Neugarten, Moore, and Lowe, 1968, p. 22). People who do not follow this timetable are often regarded as deviant; the adult who returns to school may be treated with contempt, amusement, or hostility.

I am just beginning to collect data from enrolled adult students about academic experiences they have found discriminatory. Earlier, it became clear to me that counselors, like people in general, often have deeply ingrained notions as to what is appropriate or inappropriate for their clients. A study of counselors' attitudes revealed that adults in an educational setting have less than a 50-50 chance of encountering a university counselor who is not age-biased (Schlossberg and Troll, 1976). Extrapolating from such studies, we can assume that adult women students will face serious—and in some cases insurmountable—problems in returning to school. Age bias is not only hampering individual development but also robbing society of productive members.

BARRIER 2: LIMITED SUPPORT SERVICES

If opportunities for lifelong learning are to be meaningful, they must be accompanied by the provision of support services such as counseling, advising, child care, and career guidance. Unfortunately, such support services are currently inadequate. Two recent studies dramatize both these points.

In an intensive study of fifteen continuing education programs for women, Helen Astin and her associates found that as "women reenter the academic world, . . . they are confronted with both personal problems and institutional barriers" (Astin, 1976). Over and over again, the women involved in continuing education programs commented that the support services offered by these programs helped them make the transition back to school. Through flexible class schedules, small-group interaction with other adults, sensitive advising, and the provision for child care, they not only make the adjustment satisfactorily but do outstandingly well as students. Indeed, over half the women studied had raised their occupational aspirations as a result of their experience.

In the second study, the American Institute for Research (AIR) carried out a survey to determine the availability of support services for adults, particularly women and racial-ethnic minority members. But even though adults were found to be "the fastest growing segment in higher education, [making up] 48% of the total enrollment of 10 million" (Maeroff, 1975, p. 9), adult counseling services are in short supply. Those counseling services that are directed toward women usually focus on the middle-class, educated woman. Very few are directed toward low-income female heads of households working at low-level jobs.

But the picture is not unrelievedly grim. As indicated, the first study found that continuing education programs generally do a good job of providing support services to adult women. The recent establishment of a National Center for Education Brokering (a term that includes counseling, advocacy, advising, and assessment) represents another definite step in the direction of linking adults to educational and community resources.

CONCLUSION

Despite the obstacles that confront them, many women are returning to school. As of the time of writing, over 650,000 are enrolled in post-secondary educational institutions (Project on the Status of Women, 1975, p. 8), representing an increase of 30 percent since 1970. Moreover, as the enrollment of "traditional" students levels off in colleges across the country, academic institutions are becoming more hospitable to "atypical" groups, including older women. We can hope that the concept of lifelong learning will enable older women to succeed in their quest for full development.

REFERENCES

American Council on Education, *A Fact Book on Higher Education: Enrollment Data.* Washington, D.C.: American Council on Education, 1974.

Astin, H., "Continuing Education and the Development of Adult Women," *Counseling Psychologist,* 6, No. 1 (1976), 55–61.

Carnegie Commission on Higher Education, *Opportunities for Women in Higher Education.* New York: McGraw-Hill, 1973.

Congressional Record, November 3, 1975.

Harrison, L., and A. Entine, "Existing Programs and Emerging Strategies," *Counseling Psychologist,* 6, No. 1 (1976).

Lipman-Blumen, J., *Demographic Trends and Issues in Women's Health,* paper presented at the meeting of the Washington National Institute of Education at San Francisco Medical Center, University of California, August 1975.

—————, "Vicarious and Direct Achievement Patterns in Adulthood," *Counseling Psychologist,* 6, No. 1 (1976).

Lipman-Blumen, J., and A. Tickmeyer, "Sex Roles in Transition," *Annual Review of Sociology,* 1 (1975).

Maeroff, G., "And Most Older Students Are Serious in their Intentions," *The New York Times,* April 20, 1975.

National Center for Educational Brokering, *Bulletin,* 1, No. 1 (January 1976).

Neugarten, B. L., J. W. Moore, and J. C. Lowe, "Age Norms, Age Constraints, and Adult Socialization," *American Journal of Sociology,* 70 (1965), 710-17.

Project on the Status and Education of Women, *On Campus With Women,* Washington, D.C.: Association of American Colleges (No. 12), 1975.

Schlossberg, N., and L. Troll, *Perspectives on Counseling Adults.* College Park: Counseling and Personnel Services Department, University of Maryland, 1976.

Chapter 15

Education as Recreation

Evaline P. Carsman

Many people would find the idea of education as recreation incongruous. They might say that recreation consists of activities devoted to having fun—to not working hard, and that education means hard work and no fun; that it is school, and school is drudgery, and that therefore it is hardly what we would associate with fun—or recreation.

Another view would be that the phrase "education is recreation" implies a type of education that is not very demanding intellectually, perhaps special courses designed to meet special needs like quick "how-to-do" programs. Or it might mean an educational program that is primarily entertainment—a divertissement requiring little effort on the part of essentially passive students who, if they last out the course, indicate that the educational process has succeeded in being pleasant or pleasurable, no hard work, nothing to be done outside class, no worry about grades.

But recreation means a refreshment of the spirit, a re-creation of the person. Can education be recreation in this sense?

For the older woman, these differences in definition have particular relevance. All too frequently the only educational opportunities available to her are those which are not intellectually

Evaline P. Carsman recently received her Ph.D. in Educational Gerontology from the University of Michigan. She is particularly interested in using various forms of media in the teaching of older people.

demanding. This is, perhaps, a logical extension of the sexism with which present-day older females have lived all their lives. Particularly for those born in the first quarter of this century, the expectation was that they would be primarily devoted to wifehood and motherhood — and as everybody knows an education is not required for those roles!

Before World War II, a woman's marriage meant an end to her schooling. If she did not have to withdraw when she married, she definitely did when she showed signs of impending motherhood. And once she left, she could not consider returning until some time after her youngest child left home — probably fifteen to twenty years later.

Other factors also operated to push women out of school, or to keep them from getting there in the first place. Traditionally, women have been a good source of cheap labor — in cottage industries and mills throughout the country, as well as in offices, retail shops, and service occupations that require little, if any, formal education. Thus working women have long combined the roles of wage-earner and housewife, both low-paid, low-skilled and subservient types of employment. Until recently, decision-making, managerial, or prestigious positions have rarely been held by women.

In an important sense, the educational system is intrinsic to employment. In the United States particularly, where universal education has been defined and established as a national goal, schools have performed the vital function of producing resources necessary to an expanding economy and an improving technology. To many, our educational system, up to and including professional and graduate schools, is seen basically as a training institution that is tied to labor market demands, rather than as an enterprise for self-enrichment and personal growth. As the demand for women in the full range of occupational classifications grows because of national policy (in response to laws authorizing affirmative action), so, it is expected, will the educational institution alter its offerings. It will also encourage more women to enroll in courses that require greater levels of commitment and performance than they previously had. This qualitative change will affect the older woman in many profound ways, the beginnings of which are already visible.

After the childbearing period is over, an older woman is not so "tied down" — except perhaps for increasing numbers of poverty-level grandmothers who are raising grandchildren (Hill, 1971). Such economically disadvantaged women are usually the most exploited—and the most in need of educational benefits. Unfortunately, only when the system develops to meet the needs of the more fortunate will services also be available to the poor.

What kinds of educational programs would women need? If they were middle-aged, either just at a point of recognizing that they would like to do something with their life other than housewifing, or forced by economic facts of life to add to household income, preparation for the job market would be their major concern. Surveys show that the skills of women twenty years or more out of school are notoriously inadequate for current labor market demands. As competition for scarce job vacancies increases, the need for greater sophistication in occupational performance also increases, and in periods of economic decline this need becomes even more pronounced. Thus, educational programs must serve students wanting to upgrade their skills and achieve employability. Some middle-aged women want to change occupations. Because most women in the work force have been restricted to lower-level jobs, efforts to move to higher-level work must start with upgrading of skills.

Both these groups are primarily concerned with credentials—with certificates or baccalaureate and graduate degrees. Along the way, though, their encounter with traditional liberal arts curricula will give them opportunities for self-enrichment as an added bonus. A new awareness of the arts and literature and new, broadening intellectual experiences may expand their horizons and, as a consequence, provide recreation in the process of education.

In 1970, there were over 17 million women in the U.S. between the ages of 45 and 59 (U.S. Census Bureau, 1970). On the average, they had completed more than eleven years of school—or just short of high school graduation. About 35 percent (more than 6 million) finished high school. Several million middle-aged women can thus be viewed as candidates for higher education. Furthermore, the trend of increased educational attainment suggests that future older women will be more anxious, as well as better equipped, to take advantage of educational opportunities that will help them to keep growing and developing throughout the rest of their life.

In addition to formal college programs, there is a growing concern for continuing education. While most continuing education is still devoted to improving or upgrading occupational skills, the return to organized learning of any kind can be a vital element in further development — a move toward lifelong education.

Various studies (Knox and Sjorgen, 1965; Lunneborg, Olch, and deWolfe, 1974) have found that "older students are as intellectually able as younger, and not at any overall disadvantage intellectually, compared to typical freshmen." According to Hutchins (1969), "the way to stay human is to keep learning," and the "nonworking society offers everybody the chance to be human. . . ." He feels that learning is as necessary to humanity as physical nourishment, both for subsistence and recreation.

Thus, older women's participation in education can serve to recreate them — to make them a new person, give them roles in the social world and new outlooks on life. Recent emphasis on adult education, continuing education, and lifelong learning, with one eye on the 10 percent of the population classified as old, has stimulated many and diverse programs. Since slightly more than half the population is female (53 percent), we would expect that half these programs are for women, but this is not the case for younger age groups. Both programs offered and participants in those programs are male. Only where programs are specifically designed for "seniors" are the majority of students enrolled women. When 102 retiree-students were asked in Phoenix, Arizona about their reasons for returning to school, they mentioned achieving a sense of personal satisfaction, learning about new fields, associating with young people, understanding today's computerized space age, and "quenching the insatiable thirst for knowledge which age does not extinguish" (Uphaus, 1971).

Courses directed to such older women are now being offered by many senior centers, retirement condominium complexes, churches, municipal park departments, labor unions, professional associations, community organizations, and other voluntary groups. Classes are conducted both in traditional schoolrooms (e.g., high schools, community colleges, university extension centers) and in more readily accessible sites, like recreation centers in parks, housing project meeting rooms, public libraries, and storefronts. Courses are diverse: arts and crafts (painting, pottery, macramé), consumer information, cooking (for one or two, for men), nutrition, foreign-language conversation, and photography (often tied to travel-geography lectures series), art history, drama, great-books discussions, history (usually local), consciousness raising for ethnic minorities (Black, Latino, Native American), aging, retirement, and gym, including swimming and weight reduction. Other popular courses are marriage in the later years, personal finances, music appreciation, taking care of yourself, parasychology, apartment-condominium botany, creative writing, living with dying, widowhood, senior power, and lip reading. Enrollment fees for many of these courses are low; they are often free. Typically, classes are conducted in the daytime for one to three hours, over a period of one to eight weeks. Extra impetus has been given this educational-recreational movement by the Older Americans Act, Title 7, which requires that education and direct services (such as transportation) be provided as part of a food program.

So far most of these programs tend to emphasize skill training and socializing more than general learning. Course offerings are in a "fun and games" spirit, rarely a mind-stretching intellectual challenge. In fact, older people seem to be discouraged from becoming "regular" students in "regular" courses.

Many question the appropriateness of "real" education for older people. "What good will it do them?" If education is perceived as a part of the employment process, it seems irrelevant for those approaching retirement from the labor market, or already out of it. Some call it "waste of time." But those who see education as a growing experience should see that the need to grow does not cease—at any age. And growing as a human being is both nurtured and enhanced by the search for knowledge. Indeed, there is increasing support for the notion that to stop growing is to stop living. Thus, to deny learning is courting or inducing death. Helling and Bauer (1972) found that many older students who start in credit-free special courses later enroll in regular credit courses (see also Stern, 1955). A survey of 2,000 retired people in California found that they do not want second-class educational treatment. They want qualified teachers and administrative support (Carlson, 1973).

The extent to which these needs will be met depends ultimately upon public policy. The amount of tax dollars allocated for educating older people will determine the number and quality of programs made available. One of the basic problems is the means by which schools are financed. State governments reimburse educational institutions for each student enrolled (head count), but the term "student" universally applies to the young. If students include *all* in attendance, regardless of age, we can make big strides forward in developing educational programs for the total population.

Making the educational system more accessible—especially for women, and particularly for the older woman—may be the single most important component to the realization of the new older woman—one who is truly re-created.

REFERENCES

Blitz, Rudolph C., "Women in the Professions, 1870-1970," *Monthly Labor Review*, 97, No. 5 (May 1974), 34-39.

Carlson, Charles R., "Serving the Needs of Retired Persons," *Community and Junior College Journal*, 43 (March 1973), 22-23.

Crabtree, Arthur P., "Education—The Key to Successful Aging," *Adult Education*, 17 (Spring 1967), 157-65.

Helling, John F., and M. Bfume Bauer, "Seniors on Campus," *Adult Leadership*, 21 (December 1972), 203-205.

Hill, Robert B., "A Profile of the Black Aged," in *Minority Aged in America*, Occasional Papers in Gerontology, No. 10. Institute of Gerontology, University of Michigan-Wayne State University, 1971.

Hutchins, Robert M., *The Learning Society*. New York: New American Library, 1969.

Knowles, Malcolm S., *Toward A Model of Lifelong Education*, working paper for Consultative Group on "Concept of Lifelong Education and Its Implications for School Curriculum," UNESCO, Institute for Education, Hamburg, October 9-12, 1972.

Knox, A. B., and D. Sjogren, "Research on Adult Learning," *Adult Education*, 15 (1965), 133-37.

Lunneborg, Patrice W., Doris R. Olch, and Virginia deWolfe, "Predicting College Performance in Older Students," *Journal of Counseling Psychology*, 21 (May 1974), 215-21.

Stern, Bernard H., *How Much Does Adult Experience Count?*, Report of the Brooklyn College Experimental Degree Project. Chicago, Ill.: Center for the Study of Liberal Education for Adults, 1955.

Uphaus, Ruth, "Educating Retirees," *Adult Leadership*, 20 (May 1971), 17-19.

U.S. Census Bureau, U.S. Census of Population, 1970. United States Summary 1-622, Table 199.

_____, U.S. Census of Population, 1970, Detailed Characteristics Table 226; Occupation of Employed Persons by Age, Race, and Sex: 1970. United States Summary 1-763.

PART V

Differences

Older women are too often seen as a stereotype. We tend to forget the wide variation that exists among them. People grow older as they have lived—differently. Poor women are different from rich women, when they are little girls, when they are adolescents, when they are young adults, and then they get older. Black women differ from white women, from women of Asian heritage, from American Indians, and from women in other countries around the world. Women with college education differ from women who do not know how to read or write. Professional women differ from blue-collar workers, or life-long homemakers. Women who belong to large and intimate kinship networks differ from isolated women with neither siblings nor children. Urban women differ from rural women. Some women can live in quarters designed for optimal convenience and comfort, while others must live in run-down tenements without running water or heat. Some women can avail themselves of the best and newest medical facilities that help prolong life, vigor, and attractiveness, while others sit in crowded clinics for two days or more before they see an intern. Some women are supplied with warm, light-weight and attractive clothing, while others pick their dresses from discard heaps. Some women live in protected communities, while others are afraid to venture into the hallway or elevator of their apartment buildings. Some women can be proud of their aging and receive the admiration and respect of their community.

Some women are necessary and important to the economic system of their household, while others are superfluous. Some women have had their fill of child care and find grandchildren more of the same, while others dote on each new arrival.

Yet, despite all these cultural and group differences, the process of aging has its own leveling effect.

Chapter 16

Older Black Women[1]

Jacquelyne Johnson Jackson

We know relatively little as yet about aging among black women. We do know, however, that they grow old in different ways.

We also know that the median age of black women in the United States rose slightly from 1970 to 1974, an indication that more are living longer now than formerly, or that fewer are dying young. In 1970, there were almost 2.9 million black women who were 45 or more years of age. In 1974, their number had reached almost 3.1 million. The national trend toward an increasing number of older persons in the population is more pronounced among black women than black men.

Essentially, older black women as a group differ more in degree than in kind from other older women who are not black. In comparison to black and white men and white women, the socioeconomic status of black women remains lower (Jackson, 1973b). It is unlikely that black women will achieve educational and economic parity with black and white men and white women by the end of this century. This paper, however, is not concerned with race/sex comparisons. Instead, it concentrates largely upon

Jacquelyne Johnson Jackson, Ph.D., is a sociologist at the Duke University Medical Center, specializing in the aging of black Americans. She is widely known both for her research and for her active leadership in professional organizations.

---

[1]Modification of "The Plight of Older Black Women in the United States," *The Black Scholar*, 7 (1976), 47–55.

some demographic and familial characteristics of contemporary older black women.

THE PHYSICAL ENVIRONMENT

About one-half of older black women reside in homes owned by them or their families. Most of these homes were built many years ago. During the past decade or so, there has been a slight increase in occupancy of newer homes or of living in apartments.

By 1970, almost all who lived outside the South had hot and cold running water, indoor flush toilets, and bathtubs or showers. There were also dramatic increases in plumbing facilities in the South, though by 1970 one-third of the older black women in the South still lacked indoor plumbing. The older the woman, the more likely she is to be without.

Only about 15 percent had air conditioning in 1970, but on the other hand, 90 to 95 percent had a television set.

Only about one-third have access to an automobile (i.e., someone in their household owns one), though this is more likely to be the younger women. The very old, again, are the worst off.

INCOME AND WORK

Active labor force participation decreased over time for older black women. Among those still employed, fewer used public transportation (particularly outside the south), and fewer walked to work (particularly in the South). Fewer reported doing paid labor at home (such as "taking in laundry").

Widowhood may well have contributed to increases in the number who were the chief wage-earners for their families. In any case, in 1970, about one-half of these older black women living in families were the chief family breadwinners, though their income was as meager in 1970 as ten years earlier. Thus, their economic situation had essentially worsened over time. Poverty is greater in the South. There, about three-fourths of the women over 64 years of age and about one-half under that age had total individual incomes under $2,000 in 1969.

One slight, but important, trend is a decrease in the proportion of women over 65 who are without any income at all. Since 1973, of course, elderly black women, as other elderly, do have the guarantee of a minimum income under the federal Supplemental Security Income (SSI) program.

Another slight but emergent pattern is an increase in the proportion of older black women in higher-income groups. Curiously, greater increases occurred in the South than out of it. However, some of these increases may have been due to increases in the earnings of younger family members with whom they reside.

Many older black women who spent their lives in poverty frequently become poorer still in their last years. In that sense, they do not differ from other older Americans. We do not know to what extent their acquired skills for coping with poverty help them.

Finally, the median educational level among older black women is greater now than it was in the past. Thus, by the turn of the next century, most older black women should be at least high school graduates. They may also have greater occupational diversity and improved pensions and other forms of insurance.

THE FAMILY

Fewer and fewer older black women are married and living with husbands. For example, 13 percent fewer Southern women between 45 and 54 lived with a husband in 1970 than in 1960. More were living in female-headed households or alone. And more lived in institutions such as homes for the aged. While in 1960, many fewer Southern old black women lived in institutions than the rest of the population (only 1 percent as compared with 4 percent), by 1970 the proportion of those over 65 who lived in such group settings was similar to the American population as a whole. In fact, outside the South more were institutionalized (8 percent).

There are more older black widows than widowers, a pattern also characteristic of whites. But black women become widows earlier. Black men typically die earlier than white men. As a partial consequence of marital disruption, as well as increased longevity, more and more older black women are living without a husband in their later years. It is widely believed that they live with their children. But this is not so. The majority either live with their husband or alone. In other words, living with children is no more the modal pattern among older black mothers than older white mothers.

A sharp contrast in fertility is seen between white and black women who are now old. In 1970, one-fourth of all older black women had never given birth. However, fertility data for younger black women suggest that this is changing. In the future, fewer will be childless. In addition, fewer of those who become mothers will have seen all of their children die before their own death. Consequently, there will be more older black women with adult children, and perhaps grandchildren, over the next several decades.

In a series of studies (Jackson 1971a; 1971b; 1972; 1972b), I examined some familial and kinship relationships among Southern older black women. I found wide diversity, influenced by socioeconomic, marital, and health statuses, as well as number and sex of offspring. Again, I found that family relations among older black women are generally congruent with those found by other researchers for the American population in general (see, e.g., Shanas, 1968).

The older black women I studied typically depended upon their own families as a primary source for both help and love. If they were married and living with their husband, they were most likely to have interdependent, supportive relationships. Those with children tended to focus upon their oldest daughter (again like most other older parents in the Western world). On the other hand, older black mothers without a husband were significantly more likely to depend upon their youngest children than were those with a husband. Older women who have neither husband nor children generally turn to their siblings, and, in the absence of any such relatives, upon other relatives, make-believe kin, or friends.

Most of the older black women I interviewed preferred, like a majority of other older American women, to live alone. If they had children or grandchildren, they enjoyed close association or contact with them, but believed in "intimacy at a distance." Many favored adult living settings, and believed that older parents should strive to achieve adult-to-adult relationships with their grown children. Nevertheless, they indicated that they often provided advice to their grown children, even when those children had not asked for such advice. This pattern was more typical among middle- than among lower-class mothers.

Although the majority of older black women increasingly believe that the federal government has an obligation to ensure them adequate financial support, they also believe that family members have major obligations to aid and assist each other. Yet the warmth and closeness of their relationships with their immediate kin were better when help was minimal, for example, when sons and daughters took full responsibility for care of their own children, not their parents.

When Lopata (1973) investigated 52 black and 244 white widows in Chicago in 1968, she concluded that an enduring kinship structure was no more characteristic of the black widows than of the white. She also found considerable structural similarity between the two groups. But she did report a number of attitudinal differences. For example, fewer black widows judged their deceased husbands as good, fewer thought their marriages were above average, and fewer expressed any desire for male companionship. Since the two groups were not comparable in other indexes, it is hard to tell how reliable these differences in attitude are. I found a different picture.

The widows I studied did not consider themselves better off than when their husbands were living. Many were lonely, precisely because they missed them. They were no different from white widows in grieving.

HEALTH

The ten leading primary causes of death (i.e., *diseases of the heart, cerebrovascular diseases, malignant neoplasms, diabetes mellitus, influenza and pneumonia, arteriosclerosis, accidents, hypertensive diseases exclusive of heart or renal, nephritis and nephrosis, infective and parasitic diseases*) generally remained constant over time and age. About 40 percent of the deaths could be accounted for by diseases of the heart. The additions of cerebrovascular diseases and malignant neoplasms accounted for almost three-fourths of the deaths of these older black women. Therefore, three out of every four black women died from one of the same three leading causes of death as the total American population.

Although considerable similarities exist between the major causes of death for these older black women and for the total population of the United States, there are some differences, varying by the time they were born and grew up. For example, those born

about 1890 have a disproportionately high chance of dying of heart
or vascular disease, diabetes mellitus, and influenza and
pneumonia. Suicide is extremely infrequent among these women.
However, there has been a trend toward increased homicide, as well
as cirrhosis of the liver. If the socioeconomic status of black women
improves in the decades ahead, it is also likely that suicide will increase. That is, the greater the similarity between the major
lifetime occupational and income structures of blacks and whites,
the greater the probability that their suicidal patterns will resemble
each other. Some preliminary data about menopause in black
women (Jackson and Walls, 1976) reemphasize the diversity of
aging patterns. Few were distressed about the menopause. Those
who were the most distressed were those who also reported abortion
histories. Education and successful menopausal adjustment were, as
expected, positively correlated. Some of the married women reported
less sex desire during and after the menopause, while others reported
heightened desire. The sample was too small (51 women) to ferret
out the distinguishing characteristics of these two groups. Further,
the correlation between an expectation of menopausal symptoms and
the actual occurrence of those symptoms was positive and very strong.
Women who reported earlier menstrual problems were also most
likely to report menopausal problems. Finally, there appeared to be
an intergenerational connection between menopausal behaviors.
That is, daughters may well have imitated their mothers or grandmothers.

What I believe is becoming a dangerous trend is the increasing
pulls upon older black women to belong to a multiplicity of
organizations devoted to blacks, to women, to the elderly, and so
on. Carried to the logical conclusion, various public and private
policies now in vogue could eventually have black older women,
who are in poor health and poor, segregated on the basis of their
race, age, sex, health, and poverty statuses. Encouragement of
organizational proliferation on the basis of these traits, abetted by
federal support, could subject these women to pressures to become
members of organizations for blacks, for the elderly, for women, for
better consumerism in health, for welfare rights, for black
organizations devoted to the elderly, for black organizations
devoted to elderly women, for black organizations devoted to elderly women emphasizing improved health consumerism for individuals who are below the poverty level, *und so weiter, ad*

nauseum. Such a proliferation of membership is probably far beyond the organizational energies of any individual. Perhaps a greater crisis is the reduced emphasis upon the commonality of critical probems shared by older and younger blacks, female and male.

SUMMARY

The underlying thesis of this paper about older black women is the paucity of gerontological knowledge about them. The problem is also complicated by inadequate methodologies for determining the precise impacts of race upon aging. Yet it is highly likely that significant improvements will occur within the gerontological literature about older black women in the future for several different reasons. One important reason is the sheer increase in the presence of older black women within the American society.

Some of the trends in the physical and income/work environments of older black women are progressive, others are regressive. By the end of the century, virtually all older black women will have at least minimal access to physical comforts currently regarded as necessary for minimal living. But their income levels are likely to remain relatively low in comparison with other major race-sex groups within the United States. Important, however, is the fact that more of their concerns will be shifting toward the quality, and not the quantity of life.

REFERENCES

Jackson, Jacquelyne J., "Aged Blacks: A Potpourri towards the Reduction of Racial Inequities," *Phylon,* 32 (1971), 260-80. (a)

––––––, "Sex and Social Class Variations in Black Adult Parent-Adult Child Relationships," *Aging and Human Development,* 2 (1971), 96-107. (b)

––––––, "Marital Life Among Aged Blacks," *The Family Coordinator,* 21 (1972), 21-27. (a)

––––––, "Comparative Life Styles and Family and Friend Relationships Among Older Black Women," *The Family Coordinator,* 21 (1972). (b) Reprinted in *Non-Traditional Family Forms in the 1970's,* ed.

Marvin B. Sussman, pp. 109-17. Minneapolis: National Council on Family Relations, 1973. (a)

————, "Black Women in a Racist Society," in *Racism and Mental Health*, ed. Charles Willie, Bernard Kramer, and Bertram Brown. Pittburgh: University of Pittsburgh Press, 1973. (b)

Jackson, Jacquelyne J., and Bertram E. Walls, "Perceptions of Postmenopausal Black Women Toward the Menopause," paper presented at the 1976 annual meeting of the Society for the Study of Applied Anthropology, St. Louis, Missouri.

Lopata, Helena Z., "Social Relations of Black and White Widowed Women in a Northern Metropolis," *The American Journal of Sociology*, 78 (1973), 1003-10.

Shanas, Ethel, et al., *Old People in Three Industrial Societies*. New York: Atherton Press, 1968.

U.S. Department of Health, Education and Welfare, Public Health Service, *Vital Statistics of the United Stated, 1961*. Vol. II, *Mortality*, Part A. Washington, D.C.: U.S. Government Printing Office, 1964.

U.S. Department of Health, Education and Welfare, Public Health Service, *Vital Statistics of the United States, 1971*. Vol. II, *Mortality*, Part A. Rockville, Md.: National Center for Health Statistics, 1975.

Chapter 17

Jewish-American Grandmothers

Mildred Seltzer

The quality of aging is not uniform. It is different for blacks and whites, for middle and working class, and for members of different ethnic groups. The present discussion looks at the manner in which the present generation of old Jewish women changed from the "jewels" of the Eastern European "shtetls" to the Mother Portnoys of their American older years, from the self-sacrificing "mamehs" to indulgent, but complaining "bubehs" (grandmothers).

In the segregated "shtetls" from which many current old Jewish women came, the "mameh" was described as a woman of valor whose price was above that of rubies. She was responsible for coping with the everyday world. She ran the business while her husband studied, and she was the source of strength for their family. She took care of the secular sphere while he took care of the sacred world. When she came to this country, she changed only in the ways in which she went about her tasks. She worked in the sweat shops, saw to it that her children were educated, and helped her husband in a thousand ways. How then did this young woman of determination, hard work, and courage develop into Mother Portnoy, the old

Mildred Seltzer, Ph.D., is Associate Provost for Special Programs at Miami University, Oxford, Ohio; Assistant Director of Scripps Foundation Gerontology Center; and on the faculty of the Department of Sociology and Anthropology at Miami University. She is co-author with Robert Atchley of *Sociology of Aging*.

woman of complaint (see Bart, 1970)? Somehow, in the transition, she became a harsh overbearing caricature of what she had once been. The "mameh" of chicken soup and chopped livers became the "bubeh" of brisket and depression. Bart attributes the high incidence of menopausal depression among Jewish women directly to their earlier maternal martyrdom. Why should this be so?

Most of today's Jews over 70 — and most of these are women — are foreign-born. Eighty-five percent of all Jewish women over 65 have less than high school education. There are proportionately more older women in the Jewish population than in the population as a whole. Approximately 11 percent of American Jews are 65 or older as compared with less than 10 percent for the total population. Like most American families, though, few (only 7 percent) have three generations living in the same household. Also, like the general population, each new generation of older Jews is more likely to be American-born, educated, and female. It is also less likely to be involved in or with religious institutions like the synagogue. (It might be interesting to learn how involved such people are with senior center programs and whether these are replacing the synagogue as activity centers.)

Hyman (1974) says of the shtetl woman, "Her role as household manager, self-sacrificing wife and mother, and supplementary breadwinner was respected, and the Jewish *baleboste* [housewife who could make a meal from one potato] became a legendary figure." Blau (1967) states, "For all their warmth and indulgence, *yiddishe mamehs* were demanding, determined women who spared neither themselves nor their husbands and children. Their standards and expectations were extremely high, and they insisted on 'the best' whether they were shopping for food or selecting a doctor. . . ."

Because studies of personality over the life course suggest that people tend to follow much the same patterns (Neugarten, 1968; Maas and Kuypers, 1974), the old Jewish woman would be expected to maintain a demanding, even nagging relationship with her children, in contrast with the more controlled behavior of other grandmothers. She would be highly expressive in conversation, in clothing, in housing decor, in eating and cooking patterns, in jewelry. She would continue to be competitive about her children and we would expect that one of her chief topics of conversation would be the successes of her children, grandchildren, and "God willing," her great-grandchildren, particularly sons, grandsons, and great-grandsons. They should have the best of everything, especially in food, but be expected to reciprocate by achieving academically and financially, so that she could be proud of them. She would come for visits armed with chopped liver made with chicken fat, chopped herring, and knishes. Where once she intoned "ess, ess, mein kind," now she urges "eat, eat, my grandchild."

The family is the center of the Jewish woman's social life. It is the arena of her hopes and fears. It provides her with her ties to the broader ethnic community, setting the boundaries and roadways of Jewish geography by which she locates people both socially and physically. "Oh, you're going to Lubbock, Texas. My son-in-law's mother has a cousin who lives there. Maybe you could call him — he's single and about your daughter's age."

Because marriage is considered an essential aspect of life for Jews of all denominations, the impact of widowhood among Jewish women is particularly devastating. A widow is truly alone because she was only part of a person and there is no expectation of a joint life after death because "dead is dead." At the same time, the emphasis upon family relationships leads to her eventually adapting and reknitting the family fabric.

Because the Jewish men to whom these women were married often worked in their own business, frequently on a hand-to-mouth basis, and were not covered by private pension plans, many Jewish widows of today find themselves poor. This is particularly hard to bear because as Wershow (1966, p. 201) suggests, they "feel stigmatized that the whole world can witness that their husbands did not leave them provided for and they must work."

On the basis of what we know about mother-child relationships among Jews, we speculate that it would be extremely difficult for older Jewish women to accept support from a child. An occasional gift is one thing, but regular support is frowned upon as something that makes the parent dependent upon the child, when it should be the other way around. They would be reluctant to accept money from their children because, after all, one gives to children, one does not accept from them. Having stressed the importance of good food and cooking big meals, they are now faced with the necessity to cut back both on quality and quantity of food. When their children were small, they could not indulge themselves because of the children. Now they cannot because they do not have enough money. However, they were never ones to accept martyrdom with quiet fortitude. They scream out their distress.

The older Jewish woman who has a husband, however, can truly enjoy the "fruits of old age." She has a companion, someone to look after who, in turn, looks after her. The adjustment to having a retired husband at home, which is difficult for many wives of retired men, may not be so difficult for those who used to work alongside their husband in the family business. There is some evidence also that husbands share household activities (Wershow, 1966).

Unlike other older American women who accept their doctor's words as gospel and who keep "a stiff upper lip," older Jewish women are known to complain about medical care. They insinuate that the doctor is not as well-informed as he should be and express general dissatisfaction with the world around them. If Rabbi Levi-Yitzchok of Berdetchev could complain to God and call Him to task for mistreating His Chosen People, then certainly a woman can complain about inadequate medical care from a poorly trained doctor, even if he is Jewish.

Physical appearance and strength are not nearly so important to Jews as they are to non-Jews. Machismo, according to Hyman (1974) was never a characteristic of Jewish society. In fact, the attractive shtetl Jew was the student, with pale face and rounded shoulders. By the same token, the Jewish woman did not have to be a sex symbol. Sex was an integral part of life and women did not need to decorate their body in order to call attention to their sexuality. When Tevya in *Fiddler on the Roof* sings "If I Were A Rich Man," he wants to dress his wife not in order to make her more attractive, but to show he has succeeded. In the United States, wives' minks, flashy diamonds, and clanging charm bracelets are the same success symbols. Physical signs of aging should not be so threatening to women who neither are considered by others nor see themselves primarily as sex objects. Traditional Jewish women are less upset with changes in physical appearance than are their non-Jewish sisters.

In a current wave of nostalgia, the grandchildren of these immigrant old Jews may be returning to their "fountains of age" to learn about their traditions and their past. They even look like their grandparents did when they were young, returning to the beards, the wigs, and the turn-of-the-century European clothes. Attic throwaways are the *haute couture* of the young; the young wear the clothes of the old and the old those of the young.

The issue of intergenerational continuity and change is particularly interesting for immigrant populations and certainly a large proportion of today's older Jews are either foreign born or first generation Americans. The adjustments which the immigrant generation had to make throughout life set it apart from its nonimmigrant children and grandchildren. Old women, whether Jewish, Polish, or Italian—or even blacks from the rural South—may have more in common with each other than they have with the younger members of their own family. They had to change, to accommodate to new traditions and beliefs. The strength that made it possible for them to survive until old age in the midst of a hostile environment may be the very characteristic upon which negative stereotypes are based.

REFERENCES

Bart, Pauline, "Mother Portnoy's Complaints," *Transaction*, 8, No. 1 & 2 (1970), 69-74.

Blau, Zena Smith, "In Defense of the Jewish Mother," in *The Ghetto and Beyond*, ed. Peter I. Rose. New York: Quadrangle/New York Times Book Co., 1969.

Hyman, Paula, "Is it Kosher to be Feminist? Jewish Theology: What's in it For, and Against, Us?", *Ms.*, 3, No. 1 (1974).

Maas, Henry S., and Joseph A. Kuypers, *From Thirty to Seventy: A Forty-Year Longitudinal Study of Adult Life Styles and Personality*, pp. 173, 197-199, 202-204. San Francisco: Jossey-Bass Publishers, 1974.

Neugarten, Bernice L., *Middle Age and Aging: A Reader in Social Psychology*, pp. 176-77. Chicago: University of Chicago Press, 1968.

Wershow, Harold J., "The Older Jews of Albany Park — Some Aspects of a Subculture of the Aged and its Interaction with a Gerontological Research Project," *The Gerontologist*, 4 (1966), 198-202.

Chapter 18

Sexuality, Power, and Freedom Among "Older" Women

Constantina Safilios-Rothschild

There is no news in the statement that women have been more restricted than men. This has been true in many societies, today and in the past. This is because men have needed to control women's sexuality — and I am referring to more than reproductive consequences. It seems to me that wherever men view women primarily as potential sex partners, they are bound to face uncomfortable tensions whenever they interact with them — tensions that can be released only through sexual activity. And since such interminable preoccupation with sexual activity can interfere with the ordinary affairs of life, women judged to be sexually attractive would better be kept in control so that social order can be maintained and social structures can continue to function (Mernissi, 1975; Safilios-Rothschild, 1977.)

Furthermore, it seems to me that men have long realized that women's physcial capacity for sexuality does not decrease with age the way men's does, and that this knowledge is threatening. To remove this threat, then, men have had to extend their power in all domains and subjugate women. They could find it easier to handle their desire for and their dependence on women's sexuality, as well

Constantina Safilios-Rothschild, Ph.D, is Professor of Sociology at Wayne State University and also Director of Women's Study Institute. She is the author of *Toward a Sociology of Women, Love, Sex, and Sex Roles*, and *Women and Social Policy*. She is internationally known in the field of family sociology for both her writing and lectures.

as their inferior sexual capacities later in life, when women were clearly subordinate, economically, socially, and politically. They could then set the rules in the sexual domain in such a way as to feel comfortably in control there too (Nissen, 1971).

In "traditional" (non-Western) societies the prevailing low life expectancy—lower particularly for women—resulted in few women ever reaching or surviving menopause. "Old" women were rare. Yet those postmenopausal women who survivd were frequently defined as "asexual." Men compensated for this ascription of an asexual status to physiologically sexual women by granting them extra power in the family as well as some of the freedom of movement and behavior usually reserved for men. Because they were seen as asexual and could no longer qualify as potential sex partners, they no longer represented a sexual threat (Bart, 1969). It was probably easy for men to desexualize older women because "sexual objects," like many other possessions, tend to decrease in value with use, exposure to debilitating conditions, and age.

In some countries around the world in which younger women may not leave their home unescorted, older women are free to walk alone at any time of the day or night, to go to bars, to swear, and to interact freely with men. In the Arab world, Sicily, the traditional segments of Greece, Japan, and many traditional societies in Southeastern Asia and Central America, even today, older women enjoy considerable power over all younger women in the family— also over younger men. They often run the entire extended family, especially when they have survived the old men. In other such cultures, older women who have abdicated their sexuality are finally allowed to earn money by gathering shrimps, or trading fish, or engaging in some other kind of business that requires freedom of movement and interactions with men not allowed to younger women. With sexuality out of the way, men can interact with them almost as they do with other men. Under these conditions, it is not surprising that young women, oppressed by men of all ages and also by older women, usually look forward to middle and old age. Besides, since their sexual experiences are often unsatisfactory and frustrating, partly because their husband rarely considers the woman's pleasure, they are glad when sex is no longer required of them as part of their wifely role (Mernissi, 1975; Bart, 1969; Safilios-Rothschild, 1977).

At another extreme, the older women in Western societies like ours are evolving a very different pattern. Because of increased life expectancy and a host of technological discoveries, many can expect to live long after menopause and, what is more, to experience fewer clear-cut psychological and social changes. "Anti-old age" technology helps women stay slim, maintain a fresh and unwrinkled face, control cellulitis, and, in general, look and stay young and attractive for many years. Hormonal treatments help them escape physiologically determined discomforts as well. Recent investigations report that women's sexual desires, urges, and potential reach a peak between 30 and 35 years of age and remain stable from that time on (see chapters by Weg and Hellie-Huyck in this book). As these findings become public knowledge, menopausal and postmenopausal women will no longer be automatically redefined as asexual. I may also add that this new type of older woman is more characteristic of middle- and upper-class women than of working-class women, though time and technology are spreading its effects to wider segments of our society. The hidden part of this reversal, though, may be that the asexual label will no longer guarantee special privileges.

It is still possible and socially acceptable for a woman to refuse to use the technological means that would allow her to stay young and "sexy" looking and to claim the asexual label, although the ensuing advantages are not always clear. It may be that in some situations this choice may make her more acceptable to men in occupational power positions. Ugly women or masculine women in business are viewed as "one of the boys" and don't have as difficult a time balancing their being "female" with competitive assertiveness (Safilios-Rothschild, 1977).

In general, then, while technology allows older women to continue to look young and attractive, especially if they have the time and financial resources to afford it, their overall subordinate status, the existing discrimination against them, and their internalized "feminine" stereotypes prevent them from cashing in on their attractive appearance for sexual fulfillment. They are allowed and even encouraged to continue to look trim and attractive, but most are not allowed sexual expression. They are still effectually asexual. If nothing else, they lack the necessary self-confidence to enter and enjoy sexual and love relationships. Furthermore, until very recently, the many unwarranted hysterectomies performed on menopausal American women underlines a view of their sexual obsolescence (Rodgers, 1975).

Look at American women! In their 50s, they are more often divorced and remarried or widowed than still married to their first husband. With advancing age, widowhood becomes the prevalent state. Until very recently, postmenopausal women who were still attractive did not have the option of marrying a younger man. Since the number of surviving same-age or older men shrinks with age, such women often have to stay single. The number of women who have started feeling more self-confident as a result of their increasing economic status and accomplishments and are able to attract and marry younger men is increasing but still very small. Most older women are sexually frustrated.

If postmenopausal American women without husbands have trouble expressing their sexuality, those who have stayed married to the same husband for over twenty-five years could have even greater difficulty. As Pineo (1961), Feldman (1964), and I have found, few marriages stay vital and alive beyond fifteen years. It is true that there are couples who manage to keep the excitement, the flavor, the tenderness, and the affection throughout life, who continuously discover and rediscover each other's sexual potential. But these couples are few and usually have worked hard to improve and extend their relationship. Most other middle-aged couples do not feel like making love and when they do, it is usually a mechanical, "soulless" activity. Trying to feel earlier satisfaction and excitements does not help. Bored husbands can find the stereotypes about waning female desires a good excuse for sexual withdrawal. They can hide sexual indifference under the cloak of decency and respect for their wife. The same can hold true for wives. If they are no longer excited or even satisfied by their husband's timeworn style of lovemaking, they can cloak their lack of enthusiasm under their "old age." Some of these middle-aged couples find that divorce and remarriage produces psychological and sexual revitalization. Recently, others are following a path to marriage and sex counselors to try to "put new wine into old bottles."

Since we presume that if society permits it, women will want to express and enjoy their sexuality as long as possible, we need to know how older women can reach the point where they will feel comfortable admitting—both to themselves and to others—the existence of these sexual needs and finding ways of fulfilling them.

This point of sexual liberation will not happen until men and women can look at each other as human beings instead of as "sex objects." As long as women's sexual attractiveness is based on perishable flesh, only the exceptional older woman will manage to attract the exceptional "liberated" younger man. Only when being an interesting person becomes an asset—as it is now for men—will older women have a chance. Today's increasing possibilities for women to develop their intelligence and their talents gives us hope that this will lead to their emergence as fascinating people, and that this may, in turn, allow them to enjoy being sexual. And to defy time and age.

REFERENCES

Bart, Pauline B., "Why Women's Status Changes in Middle Age: The Turns of the Social Ferris Wheel," *Sociological Symposium*, 3 (1969), 1-18.

Feldman, H., *Development of the Husband-Wife Relationship: A Research Report*. New York: Cornell University Press, 1964.

Mernissi, Fatima, *Beyond the Veil. Male-Female Dynamics in a Modern Muslim Society*. New York: Schenkman Publishing Co., 1975.

Nissen, Lingjald, "The Role of the Sexual Constellation," *Acta Sociologica*, 14, Nos. 1, 2 (1971), 52-58.

Pineo, P.C., "Disenchantment in the Later Years of Marriage," *Marriage and Family Living*, 13 (January, 1964), 7-13.

Rodgers, Joann, "Rush to Surgery," *The New York Times Magazine*, September 21, 1975, pp. 34-42.

Safilios-Rothschild, Constantina, *Love, Sex, and Sex Roles*. Englewood Cliffs, N. J.: Prentice-Hall, 1977.

Chapter 19

Mainstream Women

Helen Fogel

If we were lucky, we might be like Bernice as she approaches 60. Like her, we would have our nest egg tucked securely away and our feet firmly on the ground. We would be involved in day-to-day work and planning for the future. We would be confident of ourselves as we face tomorrow, knowing that whatever our gains and losses, we had capably endured all our yesterdays.

Bernice is a daughter of Polish immigrants. Like her mother before her, she has always worked—mostly at jobs that many would consider menial.

She married her first husband at the age of 17. He was a factory worker and he died in 1955. Bernice too had worked in an auto plant. She was laid off about the time her husband died and their son turned 18.

She found a clerical job with less pay, but at least she was working. In 1966 she remarried, a widower whom she met at work.

She is now settled into a mellow second marriage after a decade of widowhood during which she raised her one son and saw him through law school.

"These now are my most rewarding years," she says. "In my background we looked upon age with respect. We had faith. 'Things are scheduled out for you,' my mother used to say. 'There's

Helen Fogel is a reporter on *The Detroit Free Press*. She has been interested in the women's movement for many years.

a time to play, to go to school, to have babies.' She told us, 'God is the greatest engineer. He would not age you overnight without giving you time to prepare for it.' "

Last spring she finally completed high school at night and proudly accepted her diploma.

At 56, Bernice is salt-of-the-earth common, but she is uncommonly aware of who she is and comfortable with why.

For the white, middle-class American woman who has lived her life vicariously through the lives of others, trying, first as a child to please her parents, and then nurturing and supporting husband and children, the approach of the middle years may offer the first opportunity she has ever had to come face to face with herself. This can be a time of exquisite vulnerability. It is a time for reluctant self- evaluation and anxiety.

At 45, Alice, who is the wife of a successful business executive, admits that she is not very happy. She thinks maybe it's the elegant neighborhood she lives in, maybe she has not made the transition from the more open, friendly, western lifestyle she left behind when her husband was promoted and transferred.

Her neighbors, she says, are mostly couples older than she and her husband. She knows few of them, although she's usually open and outgoing. She would like to form a few warm friendships. Maybe moving to a new neighborhood, something "a little more countryish," might help. "I hate to think I'm going to be here forever," she said. "I resented the move and hated to make it. My husband tells me I'm out of my comfort zone."

And beyond her job as manager of the household, she feels at loose ends. "I'm not financially motivated enough to go to work," she explained, however.

She doesn't need to worry about money. Although the family spends most of her husband's $50,000 plus a year, they are comfortable and secure in the feeling that there's more where it came from.

Her single work experience came right after her post-college marriage. "I taught kindergarten and I hated every day of it," she said. "I was relieved when I got pregnant.

She maintains stubbornly—and just a little bitterly—"I am fulfilled being a housewife." She believes the woman's movement has alienated a lot of women who previously found solutions for their surplus energy and creativity by doing volunteer work.

Even beyond the matter of money, employment is no answer for Alice. "I don't think it's written that you'll find a job that's fun," she said. So she's experimenting with a new volunteer job that will call upon her interest and college background in psychology, working as an unpaid professional with mentally handicapped adults.

It's work that she can schedule around her frequent traveling and her involvements with her youngest daughter, who is still living at home.

She is trying hard to anticipate and prepare for what she saw happen to her mother—devastating loneliness.

Nevertheless, she said, "I am angry all the time—I mean really angry."

She thinks maybe women who are young now will have things a little easier. "They are better able to define life for themselves," she said. "I chose my road without thinking of the alternatives. Now girls go out and see what things are all about. They ask a few more questions."

"Somewhere along the line," said Alice, "they changed the rules on our generation."

Help

Sometimes women are not able to take advantage of existing facilities and programs because of internal problems and environmental limitations. The women we are talking about in this book— the generations of women growing older—have a quadruple bind when it comes to needing help. First, they have been brought up to believe they should manage their affairs, that it is shameful to admit to others that you cannot handle your troubles. Second, they have also been brought up to believe that the needs of older women are secondary to those of the younger generation and to men. Third, most of the helping professionals believe that older people are not as treatable as younger persons, and if they make a choice about where to put their time and energy, it is more efficient to devote it to "productive people." Fourth, most of these women have not acquired the skills and knowhow (considered "masculine") that are needed to survive in modern urban society. For instance, they depended on a man to make repairs, to handle finances, and to get services from the bureaucracy. A recent development that is countering these attitudes is the availability of government funds for treatment of older adults.

Part VI describes some ways to deal with these problems.

Chapter 20

The Nitty-Gritty of Survival

Eva Kahana / Asuman Kiyak

Two bright-eyed male students are glancing over the shoulders of the grey-haired, bespectacled men and women eating a hot lunch in one of the new nutritional programs in Detroit. They are discussing these people in a tone of surprise. One says:

> I bet it must be hard for these poor old men being left alone with no wife to cook for them! I wonder how they manage to survive?

The other student wonders:

> But what about these old ladies! You'd think they would be used to taking care of themselves and would rather stay home and cook.

Their discussion highlights the current turn of events. Instead of ignoring older people, many are now trying to help them. Community services for older people have been increasing rapidly as many communities or social agencies manage to obtain money for whatever they figure older people surely need (Binstock, 1967). What has resulted, however — as our own recent survey of agencies in two Detroit-area communities shows — is a preponderance of

Eva Kahana, Ph.D., is Professor of Sociology at Wayne State University, and Director of the Elderly Care Research Center. She has surveyed older people in two communities in Detroit about their practical needs. She is widely known for her research in diverse areas of gerontology and has written numerous articles for professional journals. Asuman Kiyak is a graduate student in psychology at Wayne State University. She is completing her dissertation on institutional staff attitudes toward the elderly.

referral (53 percent) and advice-giving (38 percent) services, but little direct help. The proliferating programs for "seniors" are usually unplanned and redundant. Serious evaluation of what older women really need has been ignored by researchers, policy makers, and even by advocates of women's liberation (Lewis and Butler, 1972).

Only recently have program planners been turning to researchers for help in deciding just what types of programs would be most helpful, and as the spotlight has finally been put on the disadvantaged status of women in general, particular emphasis is being put on the special characteristics and situations of older women.

Our discussion here is based on a study we recently completed in two Detroit communities—one Jewish and one Polish. Thus, we must bear in mind that what we found to be true for these communities may not be true of other American communities or of older women in the future.

Our first questions were, "Does the older woman need more or fewer services than her male counterpart? Does she need different services, and does she show different attitudes?" We felt that some differences in service needs may be due to differing attitudes between men and women, while others reflect differing life situations. For example, married women may show different needs from widows.

In the general population, approximately 60 percent of women over age 65 are widows, while only 30 percent of men are widowers. The larger proportion of widows may be due to three basic factors. First, women live longer than men (Brotman, 1972); second, they are often married to older men; and finally, their chances for remarriage are slim. Thus, widows tend to make it on their own, to turn to family, and only occasionally to remarry. In contrast, widowers overwhelmingly remarry—to women who are considerably younger than themselves. We felt that these differences in lifestyle should have a major impact on the needs of older women.

One possible gain in the often dreary process of getting used to life alone after widowhood may be that of increased independence. Some women, for the first time in their lives, learn how to handle their finances and manage their own affairs (Lopata, 1974). This greater self-reliance should diminish their need for outside services.

Differences in personality and attitudes between men and women may also play an important role. In the past, it has been argued that women of all ages are more passive, dependent, and conforming than men (Sherman, 1971; Oetzel, 1966). Studies of health services seem to confirm this. Women of all ages complain more about symptoms and are more willing to accept medical services than men (Spiegelman, 1964). Let us now turn to the substance of our study.

We interviewed 302 elderly city dwellers whose average age was 73 years. Fourteen percent of the men and 57.5 percent of the women were widowed. We asked them to tell us what kind of help they thought they needed and wanted, even though we knew that they would probably give us underestimates of their real needs. In these older generations of Americans, it is a social stigma to be in need and dependent on others (Ehrlich and Kahana, 1970).

We also interviewed representatives of thirteen community agencies and ninety-three friends and family members who were mentioned by the older people themselves. Finally, we surveyed the kinds of services that were actually available in the two communities.

What did we find? First of all, we found very few service programs for older people in these two communities. As mentioned earlier, most of the services available just told people other places to go for help or gave general advice. And the facilities they were directed to were usually too far away, with no transportation available for getting there. Others had strict eligibility requirements for which most of our people did not qualify. Therefore, the needs they mentioned had no way of being met. What were these needs?

HOUSEHOLD AND SELF-MAINTENANCE

Not surprisingly, most of the older women living alone, especially the widows, were far from being independent and self-sufficient. Sixty-five percent of them reported household difficulties, as opposed to 28 percent of the men. In contrast to earlier studies, it was found that widows often do need help with daily living. In the area of self-maintenance (including bathing, dressing, grooming), even though fewer people said they had problems, more women than men did (27 percent versus 14 percent).

VULNERABILITY

We found tremendous vulnerability of all the older people, and especially the women, to robbery and assault. Many reported having their purse stolen and their house broken into and ransacked. Many also had been intimidated by neighborhood youth.

> One afternoon I was walking home. Four boys came at me and started to try and mess me up. A man across the street saw them and started to yell at them. They got scared and ran. I was plenty scared, too. That was when I decided I had to move away.

Neighborhood problems are then major concerns: crime, fires, and undesirable neighbors. They mentioned such problems twice as often as any other. They were particularly upset by noisy and disrespectful children.

> Children in this project have no respect. They pull up my tulips as soon as they bloom. Their parents don't make them obey.

> Kids around here are noisy. Their mothers told me to mind my own business when I told them. I'm going to call the police if they don't stop.

Older women living alone appeared to be more vulnerable to neighborhood problems than men living alone (46 percent versus 23 percent), although married women mentioned fewer problems than married men. Husbands would be the ones who dealt with social agencies. They had the problems instead of their wife, but then they also had a certain amount of experience. When they died, their widows were truly at a loss. On the other hand, contrary to our expectations, the older women reported little discrimination or rejection either by society or their family.

SPECIFIC SERVICES

Few women said they needed general household help. What they were more likely to mention was household maintenance (32 percent) and repair services (35 percent). One-third said a visiting nurse was important, but only 4 percent said they would personally use such a service. They also mentioned legal, job, and family counseling. It is especially striking that 25 percent of these older women felt that the community needed a legal counseling service and 20 percent felt a need for job counseling. Fewer men said these services were necessary. However, more men admitted they personally could make use of them.

The agency representatives and the friends and relatives of the older women we interviewed saw them as having very different needs than they did themselves. The agency representatives stressed needs for better transportation, for legal, retirement, and personal counseling, and for health care. Family and friends mentioned services and emotional support.

CONCLUSION

Taken as a whole, our results suggest that these older women find household maintenance their greatest problem. Their vulnerability to burglary, vandalism, and victimization by youth has often been discussed.

Being married makes a difference in living comfortably and safely in old age. Also, older women look to their family and friends for assistance in time of need much more readily than they look to professionals.

The salience of household problems may reflect the importance of housewifery for this generation (Kahana and Coe, 1967). Managing a household independently is a signal measure of their worth.

As society's focus is shifting from institutionalizing older people to finding alternatives in community living, we must recognize that tomorrow's older women are likely to be dramatically different from their mothers and grandmothers. As women increasingly live into very old age and experience physical problems, their friends and families may no longer be able to provide sufficient supports for continued independent living. Imaginative services and programs will be required to help them survive in the community.

Planners should look toward less traditional models of service delivery, but think of helping with home repairs, errands, and transportation. We should stop referring older people from one agency to the next, as we do today, and instead design community-based programs to provide direct assistance. Programs should address a cluster of needs rather than limited specific services. Finally, the know-how and resources of the older women themselves could be utilized. They could help one another and thus benefit themselves.

REFERENCES

Brotman, H., *Facts and Figures on Older Americans, Publication #5, An Overview*. Washington, D.C.: U.S. Department of Health, Education and Welfare, Administration on Aging, 1972.

Ehrlich, P., and E. Kahana, "Door-to-Door Survey of Elderly Population in a Transitional Neighborhood," paper presented at Gerontological Society Meetings, Toronto, October, 1970.

Kahana, E., and R. M. Coe, "Dimensions of Conformity: A Multidisciplinary View," *Journal of Gerontology* (January 1969), 511-572.

Lewis, M. W., and R. N. Butler, "Why is Women's Lib Ignoring Old Women?", *Aging and Human Development*, 3 (1972), 223-231.

Lopata, H. Z., *Widowhood in an American City*. Cambridge, Mass.: Schenkman Publishing Company, Inc., 1973.

————, "Perceived Adequacy of Supports Provided by Resources of American Urban Widows," submitted for publication to Sage Publications, 1974.

Octzel, R., "Annotated Bibliography of Sex Differences," in *Development of Sex Differences*, ed. E. E. Maccoby. Stanford, Calif.: Stanford University Press, 1966.

Sherman, J., *The Psychology of Women*. Springfield, Ill.: Charles C. Thomas, 1971.

Sommers, T., "The Compounding Impact of Age on Sex," *Civil Rights Digest*, 7, No. 1 (1974), 2-9.

Spiegelman, M. 1959, U.S. National Health Survey, Health Statistics Series B#6, *Trends in the United States Since 1900*. Bryn Mawr, Pa.: The American College of Life Underwriters, 1964, pp. 8-9.

Streib, G. "Mechanisms for Change—Viewed in a Sociological Context," proceedings of the 20th Annual Conference of the Institute of Gerontology, Ann Arbor, 1975.

Chapter 21

Is There a Psychiatrist in the House?

Kenneth Israel

The older woman of today is pulled in several directions, none of them the sure path to salvation. New forces create new demands and open new visions of action and role, even though they may upset the applecart of established patterns. These new forces cause uncertainty and doubt about choices made long ago. The process of growing older leads naturally to a consideration of times past, often with regret, but sometimes with satisfaction. It also leads to dissatisfaction when the sense of who one is and what one is worth has been based upon the reflected sparkle of the doings of others (children, husbands). This has so often been the case of women whose role was primarily domestic. Changes of later life (death, divorce) often make self-reliance an unfamiliar instrument.

Older women, like other older people, tend to believe "You can't teach an old dog new tricks" and "I've only a few years left." The many older women I have seen in practice talk about their feelings of blank, yawning emptiness, of their deep doubts about how they can fill this void—or whether it is even worth the effort.

When marriage or children have been less than sustaining, the feelings of loss, disappointment, and depression are often too much. Half the suicides in the United States are women over 45.

Kenneth Israel, M.D., is a psychiatrist in private practice in Detroit, Michigan. He has been consultant to the Michigan Epilepsy Center for many years. His practice includes a high percentage of older women among his patients.

Not all the problems of older women relate to loneliness. Many frictions develop when the husband retires and they are called upon to reorder life to meet his new needs, frequently at the expense of their own. Many times they are shocked to discover that their husband of many years, recently retired, is resentful and jealous of some small outside activity of theirs, in church or club affairs.

In this welter of conflicting pulls, the growing feeling of self-doubt may make it harder and harder to continue to function, to enjoy life, to want to go on. The questions of who am I — what is the meaning in my life — arise with great force.

Psychotherapy can be a way to help answer these questions. This alternative is too often restricted to severe pathological conditions that scream for immediate attention and hospitalization. But therapy can be at least as useful for resolving urgent everyday conflicts or improving the ways of coping with life. There are practical obstacles to overcome, however.

Spending money for psychiatric treatment is hard on the fixed income that most older people have. Private insurance and government programs offer some help, though much remains to be done in this area. In fact, adequate health care in general is one of the major concerns of most older citizens.

Can psychotherapy help? Yes, but let us try to make clear what we are talking about. What is psychotherapy? It is a way of helping by understanding what it is like to be inside a hurting person, or sharing in some measure that person's anxiety, pain, depression, or joy, and communicating that understanding back. Sometimes this is accomplished best in a one-to-one relationship, and sometimes the support and encouragement provided by other people in group psychotherapy is more helpful. Individual factors and special circumstances determine these choices. The goal is the patient's understanding. It is most often — but not always — accomplished by words. And it strengthens and heals. It offers the person seeking help an opportunity to look at herself from new points of view and to feel new worth and new possibility in herself. Can just talking help? No — but understanding of one person by another and demonstrating that understanding, that insight, can lead to growth and strength. Why not talk to a friend or relative? Because there are so often feelings that are tender or that may hurt others, which must nevertheless be expressed. Also, training in how to listen, support, and encourage helps the therapist speed the process of change. This process is illustrated by two women who came to see me.

Ms. Z came because her family doctor had sent her. She felt gloomy and sad. In fact, the doctor had become concerned because she had begun to talk about funeral arrangements and burial plans. She wanted to die, but she also wanted to feel better. There seemed to be no way to help her feel better, though. It was not that her retirement, six years earlier, had come as a blow—she had even looked forward to giving up her routine government clerical job after thirty-five years. She had never been emotionally involved with a man, but had always felt it was her duty to work and care for her mother and father. Her only brother had moved to a distant city and seldom contacted the family. When her mother had died some years earlier, she continued to maintain their small home and look after her aging father. Finally, when his death left her alone, she kept a lively interest in plants, television, visiting with neighbors—and she was still working. During the two years after she retired, her limited world narrowed even further. For one thing, neighbors with whom she had been friendly began to move away. She felt little in common with the younger neighbors who replaced the old familiar faces. She began to go out for walks less often, prepared meals less regularly, and finally when she slipped on the ice and broke her arm, she was overwhelmed. It was not a bad fracture. No bones were out of place. But she had to wear a heavy, clumsy cast. The daily problems of caring for herself seemed more and more complicated. It was a chore to wash, or to fix a bowl of soup. She limped through the next weeks and even when the cast was removed and the X-rays showed good healing, her mood did not improve.

She was not enthusiastic about seeing a psychiatrist but she agreed after some urging by her doctor. She felt old and discouraged, and didn't think it was worth spending money on herself. Besides, she had always been able to take care of herself. Why should she have to ask for help now?

I didn't say much in the early visits but I did pay close attention to what she was saying. I remembered what she had talked about before. I made some suggestions which she followed, about changing her housing, about contacting some old friends from work who were also retired, and about inviting her brother for a visit. She continued to see me regularly for about three months. During that time, she sold her home and was able to find a one-room apartment in a building where there were some other older people with whom she shared an occasional meal or shopping trip. She began to take small sightseeing trips by bus. Then her visits to me were reduced to one every two months, and were eventually discontinued.

In this case, Ms. Z was helped to see the possibility of change. She was encouraged to rely again upon herself and to reopen her relationship with her brother and other people. As a psychiatrist, I served the role of another person who seemed interested in her, capable to help her, and understanding of her need for help as well as her need to do for herself. I was able to help her achieve a new sense of self-worth and with it an interest to go on living.

Mrs. X came to see me, feeling very frightened. Her marriage of thirty years (three children) seemed in a lot of trouble. Violent quarrels were flaring up more and more frequently between her and her husband. It seemed to her that it had been getting worse over the past six months. She began to feel that she had to let him know about some of the things that had been bothering her. She knew she could count on Joe. He was steady and reliable. He was a "kind" person, and if she approached him in the right way, she almost always got her way, whether it was about vacations, clothing, or new carpets. But getting her way just didn't seem that satisfying anymore. Besides, since her 11-year- old child had stopped coming home for lunch, she found that she was finished with the housework by noon but that it no longer seemed very satisfying to get everything "just right." Joe was pretty tired at the end of the day and the movies or a visit to relatives, which was all he wanted to do, provided very little variety in her life. She felt restless and disquieted. When she talked with friends, she found that they shared her feelings of boredom. Some of them suggested that she ought to go to work, but every time she tried to talk to Joe about this, he got angry. "Haven't I always been able to take care of you? What is it? Are you interested in meeting other men?" In fact, the idea of going to work wasn't all that attractive to her either. She wanted something, but she didn't know what.

Most of her life there hadn't been too many important problems. Her older brother had gone on to college and then professional school, but the limited family resources would have made it a strain to pay for more schooling for her — and it never seemed very important since she was attractive, popular, and would obviously marry young. This occurred the year after high school and just after her 18th birthday.

We talked about what had happened over the thirty years: the joys and anxieties of three children, changes in housing and neighborhood; improving economic security; illnesses and losses of some who were close. We also talked of some things that had not happened, chiefly her own development. In some ways, high school seemed only yesterday, but it was harder and harder to keep believing that new things might still happen to her. As her sense of frustration rose, she began talking about her resentments. Joe became increasingly annoyed. He felt his wife had rejected all his years of hard work and dedication to their marriage.

The three of us arranged some joint meetings. Mr. X was slowly able to see that his wife strongly needed to find some new pattern of living for herself and that he could encourage her efforts to do so. Hesitantly, with some false starts, she found her way into the paraprofessional medical training program, where she now is. She finds the work hard but satisfying. Her husband has found it hard to share some of the family decision making, but the additional income supplied by his wife has made it easier to do so. She still has misgivings about the three days a week her daughter must spend an hour at an aunt's house on the way home from school. She has, however, achieved a new sense of self-confidence and self-acceptance that has helped her to resolve some of the resentment she felt during the many years when she had had to put her own needs into a secondary position. Of course, problems remain despite her many meetings with me, either with her husband or separately. Some areas of her life have improved greatly. For example, sexual relations are freer and more satisfying for both; they no longer serve as a vehicle for feelings better dealt with in words. There are concrete changes in power relationships that cause trouble. Her husband is uncomfortable about her expanded network of interpersonal relationships, particularly with men. Mrs. X also still has doubts about the wisdom of her diminished availability to her youngest daughter. On the whole, though, both Mr. and Mrs. X agree that their marriage is stronger.

I hope this discussion helps to emphasize that psychotherapy with older persons using basic and conventional approaches is possible within reasonable periods of time. It should be remembered that we are dealing with individuals who have generally weathered many crises and who have developed means of coping with difficulties. The task of the therapist is to make it possible for such older clients to call upon their own inner, time-tested strengths. We should remember that crises occur later in life as well as in youth and that they can pass much as they do at earlier times. Life at all ages is a process of change, not a state of immutable being.

Finally, attention must be paid to the common problem of the older women whose chief sense of worth has been derived, in a reflected way, from another person. As the source of that illumination fades, her sense of self-worth often fades with it. We must search for ways to inspire a sense of individuality. Psychotherapy can be one of those methods.

Chapter 22

Helping Each Other

Elinor Waters / Betty White

Dr. Israel's discussion in the last chapter focused on the psychiatric treatment of older women; in this chapter we will describe the program of group counseling offered by our adult counseling center. The Continuum Center's program utilizes a largely untapped source of mental health services by training older people themselves to work as paraprofessional counselors.

THE NEED FOR COUNSELING

Think of the women you know whom you consider to be handling their age well. Chances are they have a sense of personal integrity and some good social skills, regardless of their physical health. This view has been supported by a number of developmental psychologists, who have noted that personal and social skills are essential to successful coping with the later stages of life (Bromley, 1971; Lowenthal et al., 1975; Maddox, 1972; Neugarten, 1968). Erikson (1963) has labeled the need to achieve ego integrity the major developmental task of later life; and Havighurst (1972) has sug-

Elinor Waters, Ph.D., is Director of the Continuum Center, Oakland University, Rochester, Michigan. Her training in guidance and counseling has led her into developing innovative group programs for men and women of all ages The success of her peer-group counseling with older people has led to continued interest and expansion in this area. Betty White is Coordinator of the Older Adult Project, Continuum Center, Oakland University, Rochester, Michigan. Her main interest is the training of direct service providers.

gested several specific developmental tasks of this period of life, including the acceptance of decreasing physical strength and health, adjustments to retirement and loss of a spouse, and the establishment of new social roles and affiliations with other people. More poignantly, de Beauvoir (1972) observed that "one's life has value so long as one attributes value to the life of others, by means of love, friendship, and compassion."

While there are many programs concerned with the financial, nutritional, residential, medical, and recreational needs of older women, there are few provisions for help with their interpersonal needs. Yet many report feeling lonely, isolated, and depressed after retirement from occupational, family, and community roles. Indeed, letters from older people to "Dear Abby" confirm this (Gaitz and Scott, 1975). Lack of mutual understanding and communication with children (Klein, LeShan, and Furman, 1965), disenchantment with marriage (Pineo, 1972), and feelings of group self-hatred (Rose, 1972) are other concerns.

While many of these concerns apply to both men and women, there are important sex differences that need to be taken into account. In a longitudinal study in California, Lowenthal et al. (1975) found dramatic sex differences across all four adult life stages, with women in all ages reporting more stressful experiences than men. In Lowenthal's study, the postparental stage appeared to be the most critical for women.

Neugarten (1968) has referred to this period as a time of mourning for many women as menopause often combines with the departure of children from the family home. Moreover, many women in this group begin a rehearsal for widowhood, which has considerable statistical and social validity. In the United States, life begins with a sex ratio of 103.8 boys per 100 girls. This ratio gradually changes until at age 75 there are only 63.7 men to 100 women (Kimmel, 1974). The situation for widows wishing to remarry is further complicated by the fact that eligible men receive social approval for dating and marrying younger women.

In a longitudinal study of 142 relatively affluent and healthy California men and women born around the turn of the century, Maas and Kuypers (1974) found that the overall pattern is one of continuity between young adulthood and old age in the lifestyles of men, and of more changes for women. They believe that their broader, more balanced interests and experiences stand older men in good stead and would probably help women as well. While that may point to action needed for today's young and middle-aged women, it does not help those who are already old. It is somewhat ironic that the temporary effect of the feminist movement on today's older women may be negative. To the extent that feminism rewards women for nontraditional activity it may bring into question the value of the traditional lives led by most women who are now old.

The lack of counseling programs for older people is probably related both to their hesitancy to seek psychological help and to the reluctance of therapists to deal with them. The persistent myths that they are tranquil, resistant to change, unresponsive to therapy, and destined to inevitable senility keep many older persons and their families from seeking help (Gaitz, 1974).

In the years since 1964, when Kastenbaum wrote of the "reluctant therapist" who avoids working with older patients, more attention has been given to the increased numbers and needs of older people. Yet, in a survey of attitudes of psychotherapists at a New York City mental health clinic, Garfinkel (1975) found that while therapists held generally liberal and open attitudes toward older people, they agreed on the "fact" that they don't talk much. To the extent that such a belief is held by therapists, whether or not it is true (and our experience certainly calls it into question), it can serve as a justification for concentrating on young people.

Whatever the reasons—reluctance of older people to seek help or of therapists to provide it, shortages of trained personnel and available programs, or the high cost of help when available—it is clear that older people receive a disproportionately small share of psychotherapeutic services. Kahn (1975) states this strongly, claiming that "rather than helping older persons, the great mental health revolution has only led to their dropping out of the psychiatric system." This seems unfortunate because, as Goldfarb (1969) notes, they can mobilize their remaining resources and become relatively self-sufficient when they feel supported and secure in the therapeutic situation. In other words, counseling can make a difference.

GROUP COUNSELING AS A WAY OF HELPING

Although psychological help for older people can be offered in many ways, group counseling has certain advantages. Issues of loneliness and alienation can be addressed in a group situation in which counselees find that others share their concerns and help each other learn how to develop new and meaningful relationships. Additionally, group counseling offers both efficiency and economy.

A few attempts at providing such services have met with considerable success. Older people who participated in a New York City community center gained a more realistic view of their situation, increased their sense of inner resources and added to their capacity to relate warmly to others. At the same time, the stress of loneliness and the sense of futility were relieved when they became able to identify their strengths and focus on the preservation of their existing health (Klein et al., 1965).

If Kahn's (1975) predictions of how mental health services will be provided for older people in the future are correct, then the Continuum Center program described below may be a portent of things to come. It embodies many of Kahn's recommendations in that it is primarily a preventive program which focuses on the healthy rather than the pathological aspects of personality, and on the psychological and social factors in people's lives rather than on their biological makeup. It also involves minimal interruption of life patterns by reaching people in familiar, nonmedical settings in their own neighborhoods.

Since 1972, the Continuum Center has been offering time-limited group counseling programs for older people who are affiliated with various community centers in the metropolitan Detroit area. Some of these centers have a religious affiliation, some are municipally funded, and others have labor union backing. While the Center's programs are open to both women and men, approximately 80 percent of our clients are women. This probably reflects both the larger number of women who survive to old age and the greater percentages of women of all ages who are willing to talk.

Each program consists of a series of seven two-hour sessions. During the first part of each session we meet in a group of between twelve and thirty people for some exercises in communication. Participants then join small groups of five or six, with two paraprofessional leaders, where they have an opportunity to talk about themselves. We have found this combination of large-and small-group work to be particularly effective. The large groups are well-suited for the presentation of information and the small groups provide an opportunity for people to personalize the information. In the small groups, leaders encourage trust and help to create a supportive atmosphere by modeling attentiveness, careful listening, and a general sense of mutual respect.

Perhaps this general statement will become clearer if we focus on a hypothetical group of eight women, two group leaders and six group members whose average age is 70. As we describe some of the experiences they have in the program, think about their relevance to the developmental needs noted earlier.

At the first regular meeting, group members take part in an exercise in which they must decide which of two things (e.g., dancing shoes or house slippers) they are most like. This activity serves as an ice-breaker and encourages self-exploration and involvement with others. During discussion of this exercise, we emphasize that choices still exist for people their age, and that they indeed make them.

At the next session, they are involved in a sharing of values exercise that gives them an opportunity to examine the meaning of their lives. At later sessions we teach them how to recognize when they need help and how to let other people know of their need, as well as how to respond helpfully to others. We have found that a "trust walk" in which each member of a pair closes her eyes and is led by her partner provides a variety of sensory experiences. The discussion of their feelings during these exercises encourages them to talk about such issues as fear of blindness or other disability. Being touched allows them to talk about their loneliness and need for physical contact. This is particularly meaningful for widows.

One of the most powerful exercises is a fantasy in which the participants are asked to describe themselves as trees; they share deep feelings about their body images and life situations. Finally, group support continues into the last session through a "strength bombardment" activity, adapted from McHolland's (1972) Human Potential materials. They list their own strengths on a piece of paper and then their fellow group members add strengths they have observed in them during the program. As the group ends, the women usually part reluctantly, express their appreciation of the program, and make plans to meet again.

After each of the group counseling programs we have run, many members have said they would like to continue meeting. Since the discussions have often brought important issues to the surface, we think it is valuable to provide opportunities for pursuing them. When funds are available, we arrange for a Continuum Center counselor to provide individual and/or small-group counseling for an additional limited period. Very few of the older people avail themselves of the opportunity for individual counseling but approximately one-third continue in small groups. This suggests that part of the oft-mentioned reluctance of older people to seek psychological help may be related to the form in which it has been available—that is, on an individual rather than a group basis. The follow-up groups provide an opportunity for continued self-exploration and problem solving. And some members develop to the extent that they enroll in our training program for paraprofessional group leaders.

We assess the impact of these counseling programs by verbal and written reports from group members, group leaders, and staff members of the host institution.

The general response is positive. Participants report increased self-confidence ("Nothing has really changed but I feel better about myself" or "I've gained new courage"); feelings of warmth and closeness toward fellow group members as well as others in the community center ("I've made a friend," "I feel closer to this group than to anyone I know," "I feel better about being one of 'them' " [old people]); and willingness to try new behaviors ("Who would have ever thought I would learn about myself at 69!").

In our efforts to gather information about the effect of the program, we are trying to focus on observable behavior changes. At the end of each session group leaders rate participants on such variables as how often they speak during the session, demonstrate interest in other group members, or respond in a helpful manner. We have found that many clients improve their physical appearance dramatically during the course of the program and some add new activities to their lives. One attractive 68-year-old woman who participated reluctantly at first and mentioned fears of touching and being touched, especially by men, later joined a square dance group. Another woman, who was initially so shy that she looked down in her lap most of the time and never responded verbally, began to write notes of her impressions to the group leader. After she had received several of these notes, the group leader asked her for permission to read them aloud. The group response so encouraged her that she began writing a column for the community center newsletter of which she later became editor.

The program has had effects outside the counseling group as well as within it. The director of one of the host senior centers reported a "warmer atmosphere" after the first Continuum Center program, more animated conversations in the lounge, and more friendly greetings to newcomers. A librarian who periodically visits another of the centers with a bookmobile, and knew nothing of our program, asked the director what had happened because some center members had begun to ask for specific books, particularly psychology books.

An unexpected development has been the presence and impact of handicapped persons in some of the programs, including those who are partially sighted or blind, are stroke victims, arthritics, or have cardiac problems. Unfortunately, those with severe hearing loss found the program least helpful because of its emphasis on verbal communication. Blind people were able to learn the names of fellow participants, to identify who was speaking, to listen to others, and to be generally active. Their presence, and the fact that they were able to lead active and relatively independent lives, was reassuring and encouraging to other older members who were afraid of losing their eyesight.

PEERS AS COUNSELORS

As we mentioned above, our small groups are led by trained and supervised paraprofessionals. The value of peers as counselors has been demonstrated in a variety of groups. It may be especially important with older people. In a discussion of older people's need for counseling, Pressey and Pressey (1972) note that older counselors who have shared some of the same life experiences as their clients are desirable. In our work at the Continuum Center, we have found that older group leaders provide valuable role models. It is difficult for clients to say that they are too old to learn when their counselors, who range in age from 66 to 78, are clearly launched in new directions.

Our peer counselors are drawn from the pool of program participants. The group leaders and project staff select them on the basis of regularity of attendance, ability to learn and use the program materials, willingness to self-disclose, ability to listen to and empathize with other group members, and a general emotional investment in the program. Their subsequent training is designed to (1) reinforce their already existing qualities of genuineness and warmth, (2) develop their communication skills, (3) help them learn how to assist others in making decisions, (4) increase their self-awareness and self-confidence, and (5) teach them some principles of group dynamics.

Because training is very personal, only eight to twelve people are trained at a time. They meet twice a week for five weeks. The training procedure is described elsewhere (Waters et al., 1976).

After the training period is over, we continue to support and supervise our paraprofessional group leaders through regular staff meetings and in-service training days. We also continue to evaluate their work by joining their groups from time to time. The following anecdotes will illustrate some of the changes we see.

A 75-year-old former English teacher had a difficult time adjusting to retirement. She particularly hated the age-segregated housing that isolated her from young people with whom she had shared so much of her life. After she became a group leader, she moved back to a university neighborhood, where she feels much more at home.

Another woman entered the program after seeking help from an audiologist for a hearing problem. Though she had a slight hearing loss, she was suffering mostly from isolation following a long illness. From a start as quiet and shy, she gradually became confident and excited. Still a group leader, she has recently also become an ombudsman for an advocacy group seeking better care for older people and a resource person for Wayne State University classes on aging.

A peer counselor who had been legally blind had surgery to improve her eyesight so that she could "help other people learn the skills they need to grow old gracefully." Another, generally quiet and unassuming, ended up modeling in a fashion show after complaining to the show's organizers that clothes are always displayed by young, thin people.

We have learned from our group leaders that the delight of finding new talents and beginning a new career is as exciting in old age as it is at any other time of life.

REFERENCES

Bromley, D. B., *The Psychology of Human Aging.* Baltimore: Penguin Books, 1971.

de Beauvoir, Simone, *The Coming of Age.* New York: Putnam & Sons, 1972.

Erikson, Erik H., *Childhood and Society,* 2nd ed. New York: W. W. Norton & Co., 1963.

Gaitz, Charles M., "Barriers to the Delivery of Psychiatric Services to the Elderly," *The Gerontologist,* 14, No. 3 (1974,), 210-140.

Gaitz, C. M., and J. Scott, "Analysis of Letters to 'Dear Abby' Concerning Old Age,"*The Gerontologist,* 15, No. 1 (1975), Part I, 47-51.

Garfinkel, Renee, "The Reluctant Therapist 1975," *The Gerontologist,* 15, No. 2 (1975), 136-137.

Goldfarb, Alvin J., "The Psychodynamics of Dependency and the Search for Aid." *Occasional Papers in Gerontology No. 6.* Ann Arbor: Institute of Gerontology.

Havighurst, Robert J., *Developmental Tasks and Education,* 3rd ed. New York: David McKay, 1972.

Kahn, Robert L., "The Mental Health System and the Future Aged," *The Gerontologist,* 14, No. 1 (1975), Part II, 24-31.

Kastenbaum, Robert, "The Reluctant Therapist," in *New Thoughts on Old Age,* ed. R. Kastenbaum. New York: Springer, 1964.

Kimmel, Douglas C., *Adulthood and Aging: An Interdisciplinary, Developmental View.* New York: John Wiley & Sons, Inc., 1974.

Klein, W. H., E. J. Le Shan, and S. S. Furman, *Promoting Mental Health of Older People Through Group Methods: A Practical Guide.* New York: Mental Health Materials Center, Inc., 1965.

Lowenthal, M. F., M. Thurnher, and D. Chiriboga, *Four Stages of Life.* San Francisco: Jossey-Bass Publishers, 1975.

Maas, Henry S., and Joseph A. Kuypers, *From Thirty to Seventy. A Forty-Year Longitudinal Study of Adult Life Styles and Personality.* San Francisco: Jossey-Bass Publishers, 1974.

Maddox, George L., "Retirement as a Social Event," in *Middle Age and Aging* (3rd ed.), ed. B. Neugarten. Chicago: University of Chicago Press, 1972.

McHolland, James D., *Human Potential Seminars.* Evanston, Ill: James McHolland, Human Potential Seminars, Kendall College, 1972.

Neugarten, Bernice L., "Adult Personality: Toward a Psychology of the Life Cycle," in *Middle Age and Aging*, ed. B. Neugarten. Chicago: University of Chicago Press, 1968.

Pineo, Peter, "The Later Years of Marriage, in *Middle Age and Aging* (3rd ed.), ed. B. Neugarten. Chicago: University of Chicago Press, 1972.

Pressey, Sidney L., and Alice D. Pressey, "Major Neglected Need Opportunity: Old Age Counseling," *Journal of Counseling Psychology*, 19, No. 5 (1972), 363–66.

Rose, Arnold M., "The Subculture of the Aging," in *Middle Age and Aging* (3rd ed.), ed. B. Neugarten. Chicago: University of Chicago Press, 1972.

Waters, E. B., S. A. Fink, J. S. Goodman, and G. A. Parker, "Strategies for Training Adult Counselors," *Counseling Psychologist*, 6, No. 1 (1976), 61–66.

PART VII

Power

Women have been socialized not to expect or want power—either in their personal relationships or in the larger world. Thus, they have found themselves disadvantaged—the only majority treated like a minority. Contemporary forces such as education, longer life, the women's movement, and more economic opportunities in the work place are bringing a growing awareness of and pressure for social institutions to change and recognize women's position. With women's increasing access to and comfort with power, power will not be necessarily associated with masculinity or loss of femininity. When change occurs, we discard old ways and find new ones to replace them. Women do not have enough role models to show them how to handle power in such a way that it does not create personal problems. This section deals with the traditional way women have achieved what they wanted—through charm—and examines the dilemma of women in the transitional period.

Chapter 23

Those Endearing Young Charms: Fifty Years Later

Robert Kastenbaum / Deborah Simonds

"Charm" is a word seldom encountered in the parlance of the social and behavioral sciences. Once it meant something that fell alluringly upon our ears: a blending of voices, "charms and lullabyes." We listen and we are soothed. Magical overtones were heard. The singing or chanting voice seemed to exert strange and powerful influences. A person who knew the right words and precisely how to incant them might influence the course of events. A charm or spell could be worked directly by voice-word magic, or indirectly by investing objects with special powers. Magical and musical aspects are integrated in Congreve's familiar line, "Music has charms to soothe a savage breast."

Today we speak of a person "having" charms, but it is more accurate to think of process, the "working" of charms. It is an effect one person has on another. Charm stands apart from the more palpable qualities of an individual. One person is articulate and intelligent; another has beautiful physical features—but neither one might charm us. Essentially, we know that we are in the presence of charm not by examining the other person's assets or actions, but

Robert Kastenbaum, Ph.D., is Professor of Psychology at the University of Massachusetts, Boston. He is the author of numerous books on aging and dying including *New Thoughts on Old Age, The Psychology of Aging, The Psychology of Death* (with Ruth Aisenberg), and *Death, Society, and Human Behavior.* Deborah Simonds is a recent graduate of the University of Massachusetts, Boston.

through consulting our own response: we have been made to feel pleased, well disposed in the company of this other person.

At times the charmer is distrusted. A manipulative motive may be suspected; perhaps we should be wary of a person who can make us feel so good. At other times we may distrust ourselves for being vulnerable to charm. Charm may also be associated with the insubstantial or trivial. A person is said to be "getting by on charm" instead of merit, hard work, or whatever it is that we take to be acceptable modes of achieving success, particularly if we detect a deliberate effort to catch us off-guard. We usually prefer "natural," "spontaneous", or "unaffected" charm. The person who seems to know precisely what effect is being made and who measures out charm according to the occasion often risks disapproval and ineffectuality.

Despite our wariness, we are often ready to be charmed. We expect certain people to charm us, and are disappointed when they do not. There is satisfaction in giving ourselves over to this indulgence. We are willing to forgive, overlook, and tolerate much in the charming person. This amiable disposition itself contributes to our sense of well-being in the presence of the charmer.

Developmental Extremes and Vulnerability

Human survival is most at risk at the extreme points of the life span: infancy and advanced old age. And it is just when the individual is at highest risk from disease and physical malfunction, and most in need of protection and care that his or her social value is likely to be most in question. Societies vary in the amount of attention they give to those at the developmental extremes (Dublin, 1965) some giving priority to the very young, some to the very old. It is hard to find societies that give strong priority—in actual life-sustaining practices as distinguished from public rhetoric—to both developmental extremes (Kastenbaum and Ross, 1975).

The vulnerabilities of the very young and the very old increase when either the total society or some of its component units (such as the family) are under great stress (e.g., political unrest, economic instability, war, famine, natural disaster). Infanticide and abandonment of the aged have long been "solutions" when there are "too many" young or old in a stressed society (Shanas and Hauser, 1974).

Furthermore, females are usually more at risk than males.

Most typically, it has been the female neonate who has been put to death, and the older woman who has lost support when her needs override her apparent contributions to society. In our own society today, sick old men are more likely to receive care in their own homes than sick old women (Bakan, 1968).

What, then, do the very young and the very old have going for them? Moral codes have been variable and selective. At times, the direction of "right thinking" has itself condemned infants and the aged to death. Symbolic factors also have had mixed effect. An infant might be celebrated or an elder cherished because the former is a monarch-to-be, while the latter represents the tradition and pride of a nation. Yet each might also be candidates for assassination for the same reason. The newborn may be seen as the family's hope, part of the rising generation that will enjoy the kind of life denied to its parents. But another set of parents, also having experienced deprivation and frustration in their own lives, may foresee more of the same for their offspring and participate more or less actively in their demise. In parallel fashion, the aged may be honored in part because they represent the family's or society's past — or reviled and abandoned for the same reason.

An affectionate family or society may simply love its young or old. They welcome the opportunity to express their positive feelings by caring actions. A discipline- and loyalty-oriented family or society may support all of its members even if they no longer contribute much in a palpable way. Fear of death (including apprehension about the fate of one's soul in the afterlife) may be a powerful motivating force to nurture the young and stay on good terms with the aged. But there are many infants and old people for whom none of these protections exist. Their opportunties for well-being and survival are therefore more at risk.

Charm and Vulnerability

The vulnerable young and old need something "extra," beyond the supports mentioned above. Charm is such an "extra." Did it not already exist, we would have to invent it.

The link between charm and vulnerability is most obvious at the infant-child edge of the developmental continuum. In fact, the very young of most animal species arouse our tender feelings. We enjoy seeing kittens, puppies, and chicks even if we are not interested in living with cats, dogs, and chickens. Tired shoppers relax and let a smile escape them as they catch sight of baby animals in a pet store window. There is an impulse to linger, to touch or pick up, and speak to the "sweet little kitten" or "cute little pup."

We said earlier that we read charm from our own response, from our sense of delight, indulgence, and well-being. This "charmed state" disposes us toward certain actions, actions that prolong and enhance contact. We wish to remain in the presence of the charmer. And we want to be closer, enriching the state of good feeling through a variety of sensory modes. Pick up the kitten and stroke its fur. Rock the baby, kiss its cheek, enjoy the sounds it makes. When an infant or baby animal charms us, then, it evokes actions that favor its survival and well-being. We are more likely to remain with it, attending to its needs, ready to take protective actions in an emergency—nurturing, encouraging, building a relationship. We are charmed or "seduced" into providing the conditions necessary for its survival and development (at least for a while).

The aged are also vulnerable. However, we seem to be less frequently charmed by them and, consequently, less likely to provide care and protection. Pet stores do not display geriatric cats, dogs, or chickens. In the zoo we are more apt to concentrate on the appealing and lively young beasts rather than their slow-moving elders. A similar pattern can be observed in relations to our fellow humans. "The skin that you love to touch" does not refer to the wrinkled and blotched epidermis of advanced age. *Why* we have such a differential response to the vulnerable young and the vulnerable old is an important question. What happens to convert the charming young into elders who leave us cold? We suggest the following:

1. Charm becomes less essential to survival as the organism becomes stronger, more experienced, and independent.

2. Increased assertiveness and competitiveness advance one's claim in adult society, but work against the eliciting of a charmed response. A competitor, no matter how attractive, makes us look out for ourselves, instead of lulling us into enjoyment.

3. Sexual maturation transfigures previous charm. Desire and envy conflict with relaxation.

4. Charm becomes more strongly associated with feminine characteristics than it had been before. This may be highly influenced by our society's masculine bias. It is not so much that the *charmer* displays feminine characteristics. Rather, it is that the yielding and affectionate quality of *our response* tends to be interpreted as feminine.

5. The individual establishes a personal lifestyle that influences the future course of his/her charm throughout all the adult years.

Concentrate upon the young woman whose lifeplan centers around winning a man to whom she can be a wife, housekeeper, and child-tender. Charm is an important asset at this time. Does she have enough charm to win— and then to keep—her love? Thomas Moore lyricized for many others in praising "those endearing young charms, which I gaze on so fondly today."* This was followed by the pledge to cherish the beloved forever. In storybook fashion, the young spontaneously work spells upon each other which presumably will deepen into a permanent loving relationship.

There is some risk, however, that a young woman who is valued chiefly for her "girlish sweet charm" may resist further development. What is the point of becoming older and more mature if time is the enemy that will carry off her charms like so many trophies of an unfairly waged battle? It may seem more adaptive to cling to youth and immaturity. Moore anticipates the anxieties of his young beloved. Should her worst apprehension be confirmed, never fear, because "Around the dear ruin, each wish of my heart would entwine itself verdantly still" (precisely how the "dear ruin"-to-be responded to this sentiment has not been recorded). The critical point is that what now brings so much pleasure to others and facilitates personal and social success is fragile and vulnerable. Time and age threaten to deprive this traditionally oriented woman of one of her most treasured characteristics.

Gender becomes increasingly important as boys and girls step more decisively into their expected sex roles: as boys become independent, courageous, and assertive; as girls become sweet, docile, and passive. And, a little later, men become the initiators and pursuers, and women the sought-after. This hardening of sex-linked roles leads to differential probabilities of charming others. It

---

*Thomas Moore, "Believe Me If All Those Endearing Young Charms."

is not just that females are likely to charm men when they follow a fetching, nonassertive pattern. It is also that men do not feel as "right" in responding to grown or near-grown males as "charming." Women are also less likely to be transported by the charming ways of a competitor. To the extent that men follow traditional cultural patterns, they are relatively comfortable in having a lulled, indulgent sense of well- being with women, but a more alert and controlled response with men. Possibly, women have a similar sense of comfort with the opposite sex while being on guard with same-sex competitors. Exceptions are numerous and not without interest, but here, as elsewhere in this brief paper, we must emphasize modal patterns.

Sex bias can be illustrated in another way. Throughout history, many societies—our own included—have spawned limited membership groups with special purposes and status. These "secret societies" almost invariably are limited to males. Adult females and the immature of both sexes generally comprise those from whom the secrets are kept. Men confide in each other and maintain mutual vows of derring-do, exercising power and carrying out a culture's most advanced or most critical purposes. The immature and the women remain outside this circle, but gain intimate access to individual men through charms of various kinds.

Finally, the type of personal lifestyle women establish in young adulthood affects the future course of their charm. There are those whose identity is organized around the strengths of their current charm. Others have a "counter-charm" orientation. They reject and down-value this side of their personality. Still others cultivate non-charm resources to supplement rather than replace "natural charm." They enjoy having their charms appreciated, but want other recognitions and satisfactions as well.

Furthermore, there are some women who would like to be charming, but do not believe this lies within their capabilities. They turn to pursuits in which charm does not appear important in order to actualize themselves or, at least, get by with some security.

Possessing one of these orientations early in adulthood does not absolutely predict the individual's charm and general adaptation in old age—life and the people who live it are too full of surprises. But often we can read something of the old woman's mode of relating to others in the young woman's attitude toward her own charms.

THE CHARMING OLD WOMAN

Charm and Other Powers

Old people in general, and perhaps old women in particular, tend to have a power deficit in our society (Lewis and Butler, 1972). Is it possible for charm to overcome some of this deficit? Let us first consider some of the more obvious powers by which people in our society can maintain security and bind others to their purposes. Do they work for older women?

Physical power, as manifested by strength, agility, and energy, is one basis for commanding respect. This is not usually a plus for the proverbial "little old lady."

Financial power is held by an affluent minority of old women, but, as we know from report after depressing report (e. g., Brotman, 1973), most old people in our society are struggling with inadequate or marginal income. The influence a person can exert on the basis of financial power is out of the question for many old women.

Vested power derives from a favorable position in the social system. In some societies, perhaps, just being an old woman gives a matriarch power to command others and receive benefits. However, at the present time in our society, this is not true for most old women. Furthermore, moral codes that might shelter the old woman have not proven especially effective, nor is political influence vested in this age echelon. Some kinship networks do maintain a special place for the old woman, giving her a useful influence within that circle if not in the larger society. However, this kind of kinship network is lacking for many old women.

Utilitarian power is what we might call the influence generated by possessing something that others need or think they need. This includes skilled services. The forced retirement and the unemployment of many employable old people in our society is a reminder that elders are not in general regarded as very useful. Despite her actual abilities, the older woman must swim against the social tide to prove herself "utilitarian" in almost any realm of life (Hacker, 1951; Williams and Fielder, 1974).

Physical, financial, and utilitarian sources of power tend to diminish with age, while vested sources are variable and not accessible to many. There is, then, a welcome place for sources of power in addition to those mentioned above.

Charm can properly be viewed as a power. This assertion does not mean that charm is "nothing but" power, nor that it is identical with the other types of influences we are more accustomed to regarding as power. In fact, it is the distinctive quality of charm that provides its relative independence from the more evident kinds of power. Consider some of the unusual features of charm-as-power:

1. Using charm does not "use it up," as is the case, for example, with exchanging money for favors. The exercise of charm does not empty out coffers.

2. Charm does not require exclusive privileges or possession of scarce resources. There are no limits on how many people can be charming in a society, while there may be only one winner in a contest or one chairperson of the board.

3. Theoretically at least, charm need not diminish with the passage of time. Although certain characteristics of the individual may change with time beyond the possibility of much control, charm itself is not an organic system programmed to wither or warp with age.

4. When physical prowess, economic leverage, or vested influences are used upon us to secure somebody else's advantage, we may yield or resist. But it is seldom that we *enjoy* being so acted upon. Charm is that form of power that is defined, at least in part, by the pleasure we take in being subjugated.

5. Unlike some other manifestations of power, charm does not necessarily ask for a specific instrumental response. Instead, we are charmed into a receptive, benign, contact-enhancing state which creates a general climate in which good things might happen.

Charm, then, is perhaps the least restricted form of power, from the standpoint of both the charmer and the be-charmed. It is the form of power that most effectively disarms hostile or competitive intent. It encourages unbegrudged attention and assistance because it offers the "worked-upon" person the immediate satisfaction derived from being put into contact with some of his or her own most enjoyable feelings.

On Being an Old Charmer

There are some fairly obvious hindrances in the path of becoming an old charmer. A woman may cling too desperately and unimaginatively to modes of presenting herself that have outlived their appropriateness. Failure to charm now may lead either to exaggerating and painfully caricaturing her own previous ways, or a depressed resignation or bitterness that has no charming effect whatsoever.

A "counter-charmer" may have been practicing the art of keeping people at a distance so long that she is not equipped for a delayed adeptness in exercising this form of power. A woman who has never regarded herself as interesting or charming, on the other hand, can find this a self-fulfilling prophecy.

Another hindrance is the tendency to associate charm with the insubstantial. Women may be particularly vulnerable to this suspicion, unfair as it is, because of traditional bias against their acceptance into recognized utilitarian roles, apart from the household sphere. Alternatively, a woman might feel that she *has* to be charming, because, her heyday of usefulness, of sexuality, and motherhood over, there is nothing else going for her.

Now for the positive side!

First, it should be clearly acknowledged that there is nothing intrinsic in being a charming person that is inconsistent with other strengths and resources. Charm, in fact, takes on a special glow when exercised by a person who could command respect or compliance through other, more obvious powers.

Secondly, although certain charms may fade with the years, other characteristics of the individual can take on charm's aura only in advanced age. For example, when students in a course on the psychology of aging were asked to establish relationships with two older people they had not previously known, and prepare "psychobiographies" on them, it became clear that they often were charmed by them—charmed not only by the more obviously personable woman, but also by some who had never tried to be "charming." Going one's own way without expecting help or applause from others does not seem remarkable in young or middle adulthood, but often it does in old age. Octogenarians and nonagenarians who remain their practical, competent, and onward-going selves frequently charm the young. Candor and earthy language may be seen as charming in a very old woman, even by those who are not pleased by these characteristics in a young woman. Some who have rejected being charming when younger now find their "non-charming" ways relished by neighbors or nursing-home staff. They are admired and enjoyed for independent or even "sassy" traits that once upset people's expectations of appropriate behavior from the sweet females. Thus, the woman who earlier relied on "charm" may suffer and falter when the primary support for her charms fade, but some women do emerge from the midlife crisis with a firmer sense of self—and with new dimensions of charm that are less bound to a youth-and-froth identity.

The growing strength of the women's liberation movement might be expected eventually to facilitate the personal development of those women who want more than charm. These multifaceted women should be less jeopardized by life's discontinuities, whether they are physical or social. (It is not beyond possibility that more older men will also be charmers. The opportunity to relax and share more of life than its competitive and occupation-oriented aspects can be beneficial.)

Finally, it is evident that our society is still in the early stages of "warming up" to old people. Paper mountains of legislation have arisen to provide services and protection for older people, and a variety of new housing arrangements have proliferated, to name only two areas of activity. More relevantly, an awareness of old people as *people* with needs and abilities very similar to people in general is just beginning to surface. We may see better-designed clothing for the elderly, promotion of exercise and other health-maintenance programs, more welcome mats out for older students in the classroom, more suitable travel arrangements, and perhaps even more acceptance of sexual and romantic interests. Developments of this kind will have the double benefit of *expecting* more charm and *providing* more opportunities and supports for the exercise of charm. An old woman may be charming in ill-fitting clothes, inhabiting a situation in which she recognizes she is not truly wanted, while her bad dentures rattle—but this is an heroic feat. Whatever general advances are made to favor older people should make it that much easier for older women to radiate charm.

Our society can use more, not less charm. The charm that older women can exercise (although we still know so little about it) promises a mode of intergenerational affinity that is both valuable and distinctive.

REFERENCES

Bakan, D., *Disease, Pain, and Sacrifice*. Chicago: University of Chicago Press, 1968.

Brotman, H., "Who Are the Aging?", in *Mental Illness in Later Life*, ed. E. W. Busse and E. Pfeiffer, pp. 19-40. Washington, D.C.: American Psychiatric Association, 1973.

Butler, R. N., *Why Survive? Being Old in America*. New York: Harper & Row, 1975.

Dublin, L. I., *Factbook on Man*. New York: Macmillan, 1965.

Hacker, A. M., "Women as a Minority Group," *Social Forces*, 30 (1951), 60-69.

Kastenbaum, R., and B. Ross, "Historical Perspectives on Care," in *Modern Perspectives in the Psychiatry of Old Age*, ed. J. G. Howells, pp. 421-49. New York: Brunner Mazel, Inc., 1975.

Lewis, M. I., and R. N. Butler, "Why Is Women's Lib Ignoring Old Women?", *International Journal of Aging and Human Development*, 3 (1972), 223-32.

Shanas, E., and P. M. Hauser, "Zero Population Growth and the Family Life of Old People," *Journal of Social Issues*, 30 (1974), 79-92.

Williams, M., L. Ho, and L. Fielder, "Career Patterns: More Grist for Women's Liberation," *Journal of National Association of Social Workers*, 19 (1974), 463-66.

Chapter 24

Young Women, Old Women, and Power

Jacqueline D. Goodchilds

Each recent year when I attend the annual gathering of the professional group with which I am affiliated, psychology, I am increasingly aware of a new phenomenon: the emergence center-stage in formal, acknowledged, official power positions of the women of my generation. As one whose Ph.D. dates from the 1950s (and whose years of living from long before that) I am part of an age/education cohort the male 49 percent of which now rules the world, so to speak. My male erstwhile classmates are today the powers that be, in government, in industry, in academe, and in the American Psychological Association. And what of us others, the women — in particular the trained, educated, professionally *qualified* women?

It's a fascinating thing. There have always been women in attendance at psychologists' conventions until recently, however, mostly spouses and students. At paper sessions the speakers were male; the few females were in the audience. If one stumbled by embarrassing mistake into a room where a board or a committee was meeting (the real centers of power), the group was male. This is no longer so. In response to pressure, being brought by and large (let's be honest) by the young, we women — the other half of the cohort — are belatedly, unexpectedly, sometimes reluctantly moving into up-front positions of power and influence. I myself as editor of a

Remarks originally presented at an American Psychological Association symposium titled, "Women: Studies of Power and Powerlessness," at the Chicago convention (1975). Jacqueline D. Goodchilds, Ph.D., is a professor in the Psychology Department at the University of California, Los Angeles, and editor of the *Journal of Social Issues*.

division-sponsored journal am at present playing publication gatekeeper, an important role in a scholarly discipline.

The question is, how do we who have heretofore been generally denied access to overt obvious power roles and status handle them now that they can be ours? No less than our male colleagues who are having to move aside a bit and make room for us, we are having to learn new ways; we are having to learn about being powerholders — and it's a whole different scene.

Some women professionals of course have always ignored sex-role definitions and differentiations; they barged ahead from the start regardless and succeeded regardless. Some alas completely succumbed to the pressures of traditionalism and dropped out. Of those who've hung on, most, to manage, have compromised. We exchange stories of created jobs, periods of unspecified unemployment, convoluted career paths that put Dorothy's yellow brick road to shame. But the point is that we have persisted and we have learned how to get ahead *though female*. We have, I submit, learned to wield power in female ways. What do I mean by that?

There is evidence to support the contention that women exert power in ways that differ from men; they expect and are expected to be less direct, assertive, open, etc. There is also some evidence coming in that the use of these "feminine" methods is inimical to the user's continuation in a power role. The evidence is fuzzy as yet. People have only just begun to care about these questions, and most research is conducted with a subject population of young people. Nevertheless, those of us newly in catbird seats know the problem: we learned by the old rules and the old rules don't seem to work well, are inappropriate for the new status.

For example, take what I call Rule 1: "Win without seeming to win." We could discuss others, of course — like the one that would by my candidate for Rule 2: "Be nice; always remember how vital it is to be liked." But Rule 1 — "Win without seeming to win" — is I think the key, the key to previous success and to present and future failure. It teaches that leading from weakness requires that one appear to be following, that one not intimidate by one's ability or assertiveness the ostensible leadership, that one — for instance — might well play if not dumb, at least less than brilliant, and never crow loudly, that a good ploy is to set one's ideas deliberately adrift so that others may claim ownership, and so on.

If one is guided by such a precept or set of precepts — and what successful older woman isn't? — one has carefully skilled oneself in the arts and crafts of *concealing victory*. Ergo, if one has succeeded, one now fails. Because in the new center-stage situation one whose leadership is concealed will be seen as one who has not led. If indeed no one notices what a great job you're doing, no one will suggest that you continue and no one will elect, appoint, commend you to another.

And similarly for Rule 2. "Being nice" has certain self-limiting self-destructive consequences for the would-be publicly powerful.

Thus it seems that the very techniques whose accomplished application has placed some women of my generation in line for powerholding status are, once that status is attained, the very practices that will insure a short reign. What are we to do? Can we change, unlearn the bad old ways and adopt new? Certainly some can and are, but it's painful and stressful and hard—and for some it's impossible.

I believe it is not outrageously optimistic to assume that the women of the next cohort (actually all its members, male as well as female) will be so socialized in respect to attitudes and actions in the power and influence sphere that those who wish to lead will be free to and freely encouraged to, no matter their sex. In time, then, the problem will resolve itself.

Or will it? In our society as constituted—leaving aside questions of the retirement years—power generally accrues with age; the under 50s are rarely in command. But there is a strange disparity between the sexes in esteem by age. As a man ages he *matures*—wisdom, experience, dignity, suitability for high office—these qualities form his patina for power. What of the aging woman? Let's face it, the dear little old lady is the very picture of a perfectly powerless person. "Old woman" conjures a negative image, disavowed even (especially?) by those it describes. Can the old women of the future expect a different evaluation?

Once more I ask what we are to do. Discredited by our years, practiced in outmoded arts ("feminine wiles"), we older female folk can not at all rest assured that the future will welcome our successors. Nor can we wait to find out.

There is an obvious suggestion. What if we were to commit ourselves to breaking the bond between age and power; what if we were to encourage, sustain, and support today's young women to move directly, immediately, now into the front ranks as power-holders. They have the skills and they do not have the bad press.

Ah, but do you see it? The old men and the young women together as our ruling elite. It has a familiar stereotypical ring about it. I guess there's irony everywhere.

Epilogue

SUMMING UP

JOAN: *Now, a year after we did the opening trialogue, I have a new appreciation of growing older. I realize that a year ago I got a kick out of telling people that I was 45 because they said, "You don't look 45"—but I can see changes in myself, and it is no longer just a political or philosophical issue.*

LILLIAN: *I also feel that I have moved a long way in my feelings about getting older this year. I haven't thought about it too much in the front of my mind, but reading what we all have said—I feel now that I am in a new place, that being young is finished, but that living is not finished.*

KEN: *I think this book has been a really concrete action for me—an affirmation of something. I am not simply having this happen to me, but I'm living that experience and trying to understand it and in some sense doing something about it.*

JOAN: *I was amazed at the piece that I wrote for this book, "Confessions," because it brought to the fore certain feelings about my own age which I didn't think I had. Either I didn't have them at that time when we first started this book or I had repressed them, and I think writing about them helped me to confront myself and my own vulnerability—helped begin the process of my dealing with my own aging.*

LILLIAN: *Yes. That's how it seems to have worked for almost all the people who wrote here because, as I read each of their statements, I felt we were all "coming out." Not only coming out of the closet, the way Florine Livson puts it, but coming out of our own suppressed thoughts and fears. Most of our contributors, since they are all past 20, are facing their own fears about aging.*

KEN: *One of the things most powerful for me is the articulation of the idea that, after all, aging is really like death, one of those experiences that we are all going to have. Aging is something that binds all of us together—if we live so long.*

JOAN: *Speaking about binds. I think that aging puts us all in a double bind . . .*

KEN: *We hate it.*

JOAN: *When the double bind is faced, not repressed, we can really look at the range of choices open to us. Getting this information together in one place was what made this book an exciting project.*

LILLIAN: *What will younger women who read this book get out of it?*

KEN: *Would we say something different to younger women than we have to older women? After all, they are more able to act on the changes in roles and opportunities coming out of the women's movement.*

JOAN: *Well, older women don't have to see themselves as victims. They too can take advantage of sex-role changes.*

LILLIAN: *We keep coming up to polarities. You mentioned the double bind, Joan. There's a polarity between feminism and aging. It is a different thing to be a feminist if you're young than it is if you're old. What is the essence of this difference? It is hard to know what we mean by feminism when we are talking about older women. In a way we are unfurling the feminist banner for older women and, at the same time, recognizing realistically that they are a cohort that was not brought up to think that they could control their own destinies. Furthermore, in the process of physical aging, they may be less vigorous, they may not have the strength to march on the barricades. But, we are saying, "Yes, you can fight. You can demand other things. You can look at yourself with respect. There is a whole other world out there!"*

JOAN: *I think we are also saying something else. We are trying to show the developmental significance for young feminists or young professionals in the field of gerontology. They'd better look at their programs and see how they relate to older women. Whether they are talking about credit, or housing, or equality in pay, we are saying that these problems are significantly different for the older woman.*

LILLIAN: *Part of the young feminist argument is that they were trained to be too "feminine" and they equate this with the models that their mothers gave them. And so, like all ideologists, young feminists are against the previous generation, their mothers. Now, in this book, we are talking about that previous generation. We are lookng at it from a different perspective than that of their daughters. The generational concept is surprisingly missing from this book. It wouldn't be missing from a feminist book of the younger generation.*

KEN: *When young people talk, they are thinking a lot more about the future—how things are going to be—what we want to change—why old people did things this way, and why we want to do them a different way, and what was so wrong about it. I think older people have a more philosophical acceptance of how hard it is to change things, maybe a kind of acceptance that you're not going to be able to change things quite so dramatically. I think it's just one of the inevitable differences in perspective from one age as compared to another age. There tends to be much more of the attitude, "Well, look, this is where we are. What can we do with where we are now?" There's a more reasonable and restrained attitude.*

LILLIAN: *Are we writing a book about social change from a perspective of a group considered slow to change?*

JOAN: *Perhaps older women in the past have been considered resistant to change, because they fear they will lose whatever they have in the way of security. I think this is shifting. I think the fact that we and most of our authors are close to the transition in our own aging makes us want to smooth our own way. We want, in effect, to make aging more acceptable. Young people, while they may see aging as a threat, do not see it as an influence that is going to affect their lives in the very near future.*

Our theme is positive. It has to do with the inevitability of change and being able to take that change and use it for our own purposes.

Index